NARC RECOVERY

How to Heal from Emotional Abuse and Survive to Abusive Toxic Relationships. Protect Yourself: You Must not be Attracted to People with Narcissistic Personality Disorder

Written by **THERESA MILLER**

Congratulation on purchase this book and thank You for doing so.

Please enjoy

No part of this publication may be reproduced, distributed, or transmitted in any form or by any means, including photocopying, recording, or other electronic or mechanical methods, or by any information storage and retrieval system without the prior written permission of the publisher, except in the case of very brief quotations embodied in critical reviews and certain other noncommercial uses permitted by copyright law.

Table of Contents

Chapter 01) What is a Narcissistic Personality Disorder?...5
Chapter 02) The Study Based Narcissist Theories..18
Chapter 03) Narcissistic Abuse 31
    My Experience with a Narcissistic Boss...36
Chapter 04) Codependency............................44
Chapter 05) Trauma Bonding.........................56
Chapter 06) Toxic Shame................................63
Chapter 07) How to Identify a Narcissist........76
Chapter 08) Great Signs You're with a Narcissist..………..84
Chapter 09) Are You in a Relationship with a Narcissist..………..97
Chapter 10) Why we Fall for Narcissist..........120
Chapter 11) How Narcissists Control You in 3 Steps..………..130

Chapter 12) How the Narcissist Used Mind Control to Break Down and Rebuild Your Identity..………..141

Chapter 13) The Law of Grandiosity; The Narcissistic Addiction………………………………….……156

Chapter 14) Letting Go of Anger You Are Feeling Towards Yourself……………………………..165

Chapter 15) The Solution; Proven Method to Help You Recover from Narcissistic Abuse….176

Chapter 16) Conclusion……………………….……..205

Chapter 1

WHAT IS A NARCISSIST PERSONALITY DISORDER

The term narcissism is commonly used to describe personality traits among the general population, usually someone who is selfish or seeks attention. Actually, a degree of healthy narcissism makes a well-balanced, strong personality. On the other hand, a narcissistic personality disorder (NPD) is much different and requires specific criteria that must be met for a diagnosis.

Definition according to Psychology Today

Narcissistic Personality Disorder involves arrogant behavior, a lack of empathy for other people, and a need for admiration-all of which must be consistently evident at work and in relationships. People who are narcissistic are frequently described as cocky, self-centered, manipulative, and demanding. Narcissists may concentrate on unlikely personal outcomes (e.g. fame) and may be convinced that they deserve special treatment. Related Personality Disorders: Antisocial, Borderline, and Histrionic. Narcissism is a less extreme version of Narcissistic Personality Disorder. Narcissism involves cockiness, manipulativeness, selfishness, power motives, and vanity-a love of mirrors. Related personality traits include Psychopathy, Machiavellianism.

It only affects a small percentage of people - more men than women. As described in "Do You Love a Narcissist?" Someone with NPD is grandiose (sometimes only in fantasy), lacks empathy, and needs admiration from others, as indicated by five of these summarized characteristics:

- ✓ A grandiose sense of self-importance and exaggerates achievements and talents

- ✓ Dreams of unlimited power, success, brilliance, beauty, or ideal love
- ✓ Lacks empathy for the feelings and needs of others
- ✓ Requires excessive admiration
- ✓ Believes he or she is special and unique, and can only be understood by, or should associate with other special or of high-status people (or institutions)
- ✓ Unreasonably expects special, favorable treatment or compliance with his or her wishes
- ✓ Exploits and takes advantage of others to achieve personal ends
- ✓ Envies others or believes they're envious of him or her
- ✓ Has "an attitude" of arrogance or acts that way

The disorder also varies from mild to extreme. But of all the narcissists, beware of malignant narcissists, who are the most pernicious, hostile, and destructive. They take traits 6 & 7 to an extreme and are vindictive and malicious. Avoid them before they destroy you.

Narcissistic personality disorder (NPD) is a real, pathological mental disorder.

The disease is often very misdiagnosed by the medical community and almost always ignored and unrecognized by society at large.

All people are narcissistic in a small degree. It is perfectly normal to love and respect oneself; without such self-regard, mankind could never have evolved to a modern society.

The narcissist: extreme pathological self-centeredness But NPD is a severe distortion of aspects of the self-love, deviating widely from normal personality functioning. It is not to be confused with "traits" or aspects of a person's personality or mood. It is a debilitating, pathological disorder which prevents the narcissist from contributing to society and almost always leads to destructive, anti-social behavior towards others.

A person who suffers from NPD - a narcissist - suffers from extreme self-centeredness.

The narcissist lacks empathy for others.

Given his self-regard, he is unable to recognize that any action he takes could be unacceptable in society. Shame is not a feeling he ever experiences.

The narcissist has a complete inability to acknowledge that he is imperfect; even in situations where he is forced to admit mistakes, he will nonetheless construct elaborate justifications, often internally, which explain the problems he caused as being the fault of others.

Unsuccessful in friendships and intimate relationships Because of his lack of empathy for others, a narcissist rarely has many close, intimate friendships. In terms of romantic relationships, he is rarely successful in intimate, mutually loving experiences, as he cannot accept that the needs of another person could be as important as his own.

He is incapable of understanding and listening to others. The interests and hobbies of other people are non-existent to him. It is not simply that he assumes other people in his life share the same interests as he does; it is that he simply cannot comprehend that another person could be interested in something other than what interests him at the time.

The narcissist does not recognize feelings in others.

The narcissist is so blind to the emotions of others that his emotional intelligence is often that of a toddler.

Similar to a small child, he is incapable of controlling his own emotions. He does not realize that his feelings come from within and that he can control his own emotions. He continues through adult life with the child-like belief that external events and people are entirely responsible for his moods and that he is helpless to control himself.

This lack of emotional self-control almost always manifests itself in wild and violent mood swings. The narcissist can be pleasant and fun in one minute, but in the next minute angry, screaming, and breaking plates.

The narcissist is incapable of recognizing that his violent mood swings are irrational, anti-social and pathological; if pressed, his never-ending need to maintain his fantasy of self-perfection will cause him to justify his behavior as the "fault" of outside people and events.

In contrast to society's mistaken understanding, the narcissist's overwhelming problem is not extreme self-love, but rather inability to recognize and love others as separate beings. To compensate, the narcissist creates an over-exaggerated image of himself, his triumphs and his importance. In this sense, NPD is the most extreme form of anti-social mental disorder.

The narcissist needs to control others, because he is incapable of accepting that his fantasy of mega self-importance is not true. When he is not able to exert his control over others - in other words, when other people act according to their own free will and not according to his whims and desires - the narcissist is unable to cope, and often will react by flying into a rage or escaping the situation to preserve his perverted sense of power.

The narcissistic rage was first analyzed by Heinz Kohut in the early 1970s.

Narcissism starts in early childhood most research indicates that pathological narcissism is not a biological trait, but rather a failure of character development.

NPD begins at an early age. One very common cause is parental neglect. In families in lower socio-economic circumstances, this manifests itself in outright neglect of the child, numerous hours of the day in which the child is unattended and ignored. In families in particularly high socio-economic levels, parental neglect takes the form of "care-by-nanny", in which the child has very little contact with his parent(s), often not even living in the same house as them, and is raised by a never-ending stream of live-in nannies.

Partners of narcissists feel torn between their love and their pain, between staying and leaving, but they can't seem to do either. They feel ignored, uncared about, and unimportant. As the narcissist's criticism, demands, and emotional unavailability increase, their confidence and self-esteem decrease. Despite their pleas and efforts, the narcissist appears to lack consideration for their feelings and needs. Over time, they become deeply hurt and frustrated. When the narcissist is a parent, by the time their children reach adulthood, the emotional abandonment, control, and criticism that they experienced growing up has negatively affected their self-esteem and capacity for achieving success or sustaining loving, intimate relationships.

Children of Narcissists

Narcissistic parents usually run the household and can do severe damage to the self-esteem and motivation of their children. Often they attempt to live vicariously through them. These parents expect excellence and/or obedience, and can be competitive, envious, critical, domineering, or needy. Although their personalities differ, the common factor is that their feelings and needs, particularly emotional needs, come first. As a result, their children learn to adapt, become codependent. They bear the responsibility for meeting the parent's emotional needs, rather than vice versa.

Whereas their parents feel entitled, they feel unentitled and self-sacrifice and deny their own feelings and needs (unless they, too, are narcissistic).

They don't learn to trust and value themselves and grow up alienated from their true selves. They may be driven to prove themselves in order to win their parents' approval, but find little motivation to pursue their wants and goals when not externally imposed (e.g., by a partner, employer, teacher).

Although they may be unaware of what was missing in their childhood, fear of abandonment and intimacy continues to permeate their adult relationships. They're afraid of making waves or mistakes and being authentic. Used to seeking external validation, many become pleasers, pretending to feel what they don't and hiding what they do. By reenacting their family drama, they believe their only choice is to be alone or give up themselves in a relationship.

Often adult children of narcissistic parents are depressed, have unacknowledged anger, and feelings of emptiness. They may attract an addict, a narcissist, or other unavailable partner, repeating the pattern of emotional abandonment from childhood. Healing requires recovery from codependency and overcoming the toxic shame acquired growing up in a narcissistic home.

Partners of Narcissists

Partners of narcissists feel betrayed that the considerate, attentive and romantic person they fell in love with disappeared as time went on. They feel unseen and lonely, and long for emotional connection. In varying degrees, they find it difficult to express their rights, needs, and feelings and to set boundaries. The relationship reflects the emotional abandonment and lack of entitlement they experienced in childhood. Because their boundaries weren't respected growing up, they're highly sensitive to criticism and defenseless to narcissistic abuse. As their relationship progresses, partners admit feeling less sure of themselves than they once did. Uniformly, their self-esteem and independence steadily decline. Some give up their studies, career, hobbies, family ties, or friends to appease their partner.

Occasionally, they experience remembrances of the warmth and caring from the person with whom they first fell in love-often brilliant, creative, talented, successful, handsome or beautiful. They don't hesitate to say that they're committed to staying in the relationship, if only they felt more loved and appreciated. For some people, divorce is not an option. They may be co-parenting with an ex, staying with a spouse for parenting or financial reasons, or they want to maintain family ties with a narcissistic or difficult relative. Some want to leave, but lack the courage.

Chapter 2
THE STUDY BASED NARCISSIST THEORIES

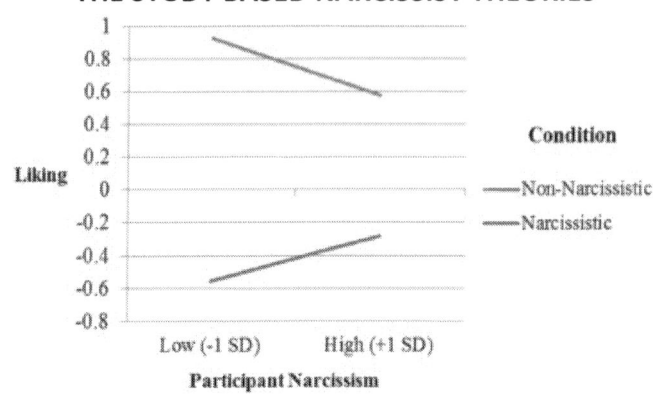

Not all human behavior theories are the same. They do not enjoy equal size and depth status. Some of them are major theories, others are mini theories, and others are just concepts. Psychoanalytic theory and reinforcement theory, for example, are major theories; cognitive dissonance theory and attribution theory are mini theories; and complementary attraction theory and narcissistic disorder theory are simply concepts. First we take up Freudian theory of psychoanalytic.

The first explicit formulation of narcissism conceived by Freud (1910, 1911) is a normal phase of development that stands at the midst of autoeroticism and object love. Initially diverse and unconnected autoerotic sensations were fused into what was experienced as one's body during this transitory period, which then became a single, unified object of love. Freud aligned narcissism with libido theory in 1914 and suggested that it eventually matured and spread into relationships with objects. He soon reformulated his thinking on the sequence of development and spoke of the autoerotic phase as the "primary narcissistic condition." This first phase became the initial libido repository from which not only self-love but generally love emerged. Freud conceived narcissism in time as a universal process of development that continued through life but unfolded through sequential stages. He recognized that in this normal, sequential progression, difficulties may arise. Firstly, there may be failures to move from li-bidinal self-love to object-love, and secondly, there may be "peculiarities" in the way the person expresses narcissistic love.

Freud (1914/ 1925) described this latter difficulty as follows:

"We have found, particularly in people whose libidinal development has suffered some disturbance, as in perverts and homosexuals that they have taken as their model not the mother, but their own selves, in their choice of love-object. They are clearly seeking themselves as love–object and can be called narcissistic in their choice of object.

In this only major paper devoted exclusively to narcissism, Freud (1914) suggested that in some cases — particularly among "perverts and ho-mosexuals"— libidinal self-centeredness stems from the child's feeling that caregivers cannot be dependent on reliably providing love. These children "give up" as far as trusting and investing in others as love-objects, either re-buffed by their parents or subjected to fictitious and erratic attention (seductive one moment and deprecating the next). Rather than relying on others' capriciousness or risking their rejection, these young people avoid the lasting attachment they long for and instead determine that they can only trust themselves and therefore love.

It is important to note, in the light of current debates within psychoanalytic circles, that the developmental origin of the term narcissism described here was only one of several concepts that Freud posed as the source of libidinal self-cathex. In addition, the paper was not written to formulate either a type of narcissistic personality or a structure of narcissistic character. Freud's interest was rather to explore and develop variations in both the development and nature of libidinal cathexis.

With regard to clinical syndromes, he referred to the characteristics observed in paraphrenics (paranoid schizophrenics), megalomaniacs, and hypochondriacs in this paper. When Freud wrote about the narcissistic libidinal type for the first time in 1931, he de-wrote this person as follows:

"The main interest is focused on self-preservation; the type is independent and not easily overawed, "People of this type impress others, being personalities"; it is on them that their fellow men are specially likely to lean; they readily assume the role of leader, give a fresh stimulus to cultural development or break down existing conditions."

What is striking in this quote is Freud's characterization of the strength and trust of the narcissist, especially since it contrasts so markedly with the low self - esteem, feelings of emptiness, pain, and depression that some of his recent disciples attribute to this personality (Forman, 1975 ; Kohut, 1971), Disparities in characteristics such as these often result from shifts. In this case, it can be traced to the fact that Freud has identified seven-eral origins of narcissistic self-cathexis, of which only one is the type of parental caprice and rejection that can lead to emptiness and low self-esteem feelings. As can be seen from earlier excerpts and as further elaborated later, Freud's description of the narcissistic libidinal type, brief though it may be, corresponds much more closely to the narcissistic personality portrayal of DSM-III than do several contemporary characteristics that trace their antecedents to either parental rebuff or unreliability. A Freud's view that narcissistic self - investment is more likely than parental devaluation to be a prod - act of parental overvaluation is relevant to this issue.

Returning to the 1920s somewhat, we find three analytically oriented theorists addressing the concept of a narcissistic personality. Wilhelm Reich claimed that at a meeting of the Vienna Psychoanalytic Society in 1926 he first formulated what he called the "phallic-narcissistic" character, although Waelder (1925) referred to narcissistic personality features in an earlier paper focusing on the mechanisms of the psychotic process.

According to Kernberg (1967) "narcissists present an unusual degree of self-reference in their interactions with other people, a great need to be loved and admired by others and a curious apparent contradiction between a very inflated concept of themselves and an inordinate need for tribute from others. Their emotional life is shallow. They experience little empathy for other people's feelings, they get very little enjoyment from life other than from the tributes they receive from others or from their own grandiose fantasies, and they feel restless and bored when they wear off external glitter and no new sources feed their self-regard. They envy others, tend to idealize some people from whom they expect narcissistic supplies, and depreciate those from whom they expect nothing (often their former idols) and treat them with contempt. In general, they are clearly exploitative and sometimes parasitic in their relationships with other people. It is as if they feel that they have the right to control and possess others and exploit them without feelings of guilt, and one senses coldness and ruthlessness behind a surface that is very often charming and engaging. Very often such patients are considered "dependent" because they need so much tribute and worship from others, but on a deeper level they can't really depend on anyone because of their deep distrust and depreciation of others.

Kernberg (1967) asserted that the haughty and grandiose constellation of behaviors that characterizes the narcissist is a defense against the projection of "oral" rage that, in turn, stems from the narcissist's incapacity to depend on "internalized good objects." In this etiologic formulation, Kernberg claimed that the experiential background of most narcissists includes chronically cold parental figures who exhibit either indifference or covert, but spitefully aggressive, attitudes toward their children. At the same time, the young, future narcissist is often found to possess some special talent or status within the family, such as playing the role of "genius" or being the "only child." This quality of specialness serves as a refuge, at first only temporarily but ultimately an often-returned-to haven that reliably offsets the underlying feeling of having been unloved by the vengefully rejecting parent.

Kernberg (1975) describes the following pointwise eleven characteristics of narcissistic personality:

- ✓ Superficially smooth, appropriate and effective social adaptation covering profound distortions in internal relations with other people
- ✓ Intense ambitiousness
- ✓ Grandiose fantasies existing side – by – side with feelings of inferiority
- ✓ Over dependence on external admiration and acclaim
- ✓ Feelings of boredom and emptiness
- ✓ Endless search for gratification of strivings for brilliance, wealth, power and beauty

- ✓ Incapacity to love to be concerned or to be empathic toward others
- ✓ Chronic uncertainty and dissatisfaction about oneself
- ✓ Exploitativeness and ruthlessness toward others
- ✓ Chronic, intense envy, and defenses against such envy e.g., devaluation, omnipotent central and narcissistic withdrawal

Kohut's Approach

Kohut's (1971) views are harder to summarize than Kernberg's views, perhaps as an advice of their greater originality. Despite being written in esoteric, if not obscure, psychoanalytic jargon and being ingeniously formulated, if at times weighty and tautological, Kohut's work has attracted many disciples. Fortunately, a score of "in-interpreters" sought to elucidate his metapsychological assertions, considered by many among the more imaginative advances in recent analytical theory (Forman, 1975; Gedo & Goldberg, 1973; Palombo, 1976; Wolf, 1976).

Kohut (1971) rejects the traditional Freudian and Kernbergian thesis that narcissistic self-investment follows a pattern of chronic parental coldness or vengeful spite from a defensive withdrawal of object-love attachments. This classical view argues that narcissism results from developmental arrests or regressions to earlier fixation points. According to standard analytical metapsychology, the future narcissist therefore regresses or fails to progress through the usual developmental sequence of initial undifferentiated libido, followed by auto-eroticism, narcissism, and ultimately object-love.

His clinical work led him to claim that the primitive narcissistic libido has its own developmental line and continuity sequence into adulthood. That is, by becoming an object-libido, as contended by classical theorists, it does not "fade away," but unfolds into its own set of mature narcissistic processes and structures. For example, in a healthy form, these processes could include behaviors such as humor and creativity ; similarly, and most significantly, the cohesive psychic structure of "self" ultimately emerges through this narcissistic developmental sequence.

According to Kohut, pathology in narcissistic development occurs as a result of failures in integrating one of two major areas of self - maturation, the "great self" and the "idealized parental image." Faced with realistic deficiencies that undermine the early feelings of grandiose omnipotence or subsequently recognize the equally illusory nature of the idealized powers attributed to their parents, these children must find a way to overcome their "disappointments" so as not to "frag" if they are disillusioned, rejected or experienced in the earliest stages of cold and empathic care. In a later phase, trauma or disappointment will have somewhat different repercussions depending on whether the difficulty is centered on the grandiose self-development or on the parental imago. In the former, the child will fail to develop the sense of fulfillment and self-confidence that comes from feeling "I" worthwhile and valued; as a result, these needs will "split off" and result in the persistent search for adult narcissistic recognition. Children who are unable to idealize their parents because of the indifference or rejection of the latter will feel devastated, depressed and empty along the second line of self-development.

They will seek idealized parental surrogates through adulthood, which will inevitably fail to live up to the omniscient powers that narcissists hoped to find in them. They are often led to be — have in a weak and self-effacing manner in their desperate search for an ideal that is greater than themselves, which will allow others to overshadow them.

Chapter 3
NARCISSISTIC ABUSE

Have you ever known anybody in the world who thinks they are better and more important than anybody else? Not only are they completely absorbed by themselves, but they lack empathy for others: the only things that matter are their own feelings, opinions, and desires. If this description reminds you of someone you've ever met, with a narcissist, you've probably crossed paths.

The extent of your relationship as well as how narcissistic they are depends on how harmful that person is to your life. "Narcissism is a continuum. Narcissists come from the casually self-obsessed to the deeply pathological in many forms and flavors," says

California-based relationship expert Robert Weiss, PhD, MSW.

Abuse of narcissism is not a clinical term. "This is a lay term," Weiss explains. "It is used when someone is very self-centered and relentless with their need to go first, be first, and be noticed." When most people speak of narcissistic abuse, they refer to emotional abuse committed by someone who is a narcissist. And it can be incredibly difficult and dangerous to endure emotional abuse— whether the perpetrator is a narcissist or not.

Emotional abuse may take many different forms, according to the National Domestic Abuse Hotline. In an effort to control and manipulate you, the abuser may constantly monitor your whereabouts, insult you, threaten you, isolate you from family and friends, withhold affection, cheat on you (and blame you for it), say you're lucky to be with them, and generally make you feel worthless and depending on them.

Narcissists don't really love themselves. Actually, they're driven by shame. It's the idealized image of themselves, which they convince themselves they embody, that they admire. But deep down, narcissists feel the gap between the façade they show the world and their shame-based self. They work hard to avoid feeling that shame. This gap is true for other codependents, as well, but a narcissist uses defense mechanisms that are destructive to relationships and cause pain and damage to their loved ones' self-esteem.

Narcissists use defenses to hide their deep and usually unconscious shame. Like bullies, They protect themselves through aggression and by wielding power over others. Malignant narcissists are maliciously hostile and inflict pain without remorse, but most narcissists don't even realize they've injured those closest to them, because they lack empathy. They're more concerned with averting perceived threats and getting their needs met. Consequently, they aren't aware of the hurtful impact of their words and actions. For example, one man unbelievably couldn't understand why his wife, whom he had long cheated on, wasn't happy for him that he had found joy with his paramour. It was only when I pointed out that most women wouldn't be pleased to hear that their spouse was enjoying sex and companionship with another woman that he suddenly grasped the error of his thinking. He had been blinded by the fact that he'd unconsciously sought his wife's blessings, because his narcissistic mother never approved of his girlfriends or choices.

Narcissistic abuse can include any type of abuse, whether physical, sexual, financial, mental, or emotional abuse. Most often it involves some form of emotional abandonment, manipulation, withholding, or other uncaring behavior. Abuse can range from the silent treatment to rage, and typically includes verbal abuse, such as blaming, criticizing, attacking, ordering, lying, and belittling. It may also include emotional blackmail or passive-aggressive behavior. If you're experiencing domestic or intimate partner violence, read "The Truth about Domestic Violence and Abusive Relationships," and seek help immediately.

Many of the narcissist's coping mechanisms are abusive-hence the term, "narcissistic abuse." However, someone can be abusive, but not be a narcissist. Addicts and people with other mental illnesses, such as bi-polar disorder and anti-social personality disorder (sociopath) and borderline personality disorders are also abusive, as are many codependents without a mental illness. Abuse is abuse, no matter what is the abuser's diagnosis.

My Experience With A Narcissistic Boss

Narcissists have an exaggerated image of themselves and require constant feedback to justify their perceived omnipotence. They refuse to accept blame, will manipulate people and events for their own self-serving purposes, and react with rage when their omnipotence is questioned or threatened. It is estimated that less than one percent of the population suffers from narcissistic personality disorder (NPD). Most narcissists, about 75 percent, are men. With a world population of approximately 6.5 billion people, about 16,250,000 narcissists are female. I had the unpleasant experience of working for one of them. I found it hard to reconcile in my mind how this woman could be gregarious and personable outside the office and be indifferent, demanding, and hard to please when not surrounded by an adoring and fawning audience until I discovered the definition of NPD about a year ago.

A narcissist requires excessive admiration and will place themselves in a position to receive it. Narcissists are experts at making people admire them. Time and again I witnessed people fall under the spell of this woman's grandiose and exuberant tales of successes, one-up-man-ships, unequaled brilliance, and self-confidence. Typical of a narcissist, she is adept at becoming the center of attention in any circumstance and can be quite charming. Early in my exposure to her I, too, fell under her spell. I was in awe of someone who demanded and received favorable priority treatment from everyone. Through my association with her I met television personalities and national government figures. I also heard her malign and ridicule those same people when they did not jump at the opportunity to do her bidding. When a television personality's schedule did not permit him to make a reappearance at our national conference, he was referred to as a sawed-off little twerp who is more concerned with his television ratings than in helping the law enforcement profession. When the attorney general refused to take her grant request out of the chain of command and push it for approval, he was called a Mexican yes-man with no backbone.

Narcissists demonstrate arrogant and haughty attitudes coupled with rage when contradicted or questioned. My initial first-hand experience with this occurred when, during a friendly after-work drink, our boss asked a co-worker and me what needed to be changed to make the office run smoother. Innocently believing that she truly wanted our input, we told her. Unbeknown to us, our observations and recommendations were perceived as criticisms of her. Narcissists do not accept blame or admit errors; whatever is wrong is someone else's fault. Narcissists are easily offended and will harbor grudges. She controlled her rage that evening, but my co-worker and I were assaulted by it for the next two months as we bore the brunt of her rudeness, impossible demands, and constant unwarranted criticisms.

Time and again I witnessed new employees grow tired of the constant barrage of boastfulness and arrogance as they began needing and demanding true guidance and supervision. Narcissists will sacrifice being liked to achieve admiration and have little use for those who are no longer enthralled. Narcissistic bosses are prone to temper tantrums, especially if a subordinate displays abilities that might overshadow the boss's abilities or indicate any independent thought. Narcissists do not acknowledge other's contributions. More than one employee has remarked on more than one occasion that a simple "thank you" or "job well done" would be a welcome respite from the turbulent atmosphere that pervades the office. She constantly criticizes employees behind their backs to other employees to insure that those who do a good job get little respect from their co-workers.

Narcissists will manipulate people and events to make themselves look good. I have never known such an expert conniver as this woman. From pitting employees against each other to re-writing history, this woman is an expert at manipulation. Anyone who questions her motives or contradicts her recollections will suffer her rage. Typical of a narcissist, she is so adept at using people to achieve her personal desires that the person is not aware they are being used. A typical example of this is her penchant for hiring people totally unqualified for the job. She sets them up for failure so that she can later belittle them for their inabilities. She also hires people who are not only unqualified but who also have personal problems. Previous employees have included pregnant and unmarried women, people with a history of substance abuse, and people with emotional problems. Those employees were grateful to be "rescued" and provided the adoration and worship that a narcissist craves. They were all totally surprised when, several months after their hiring, she no longer required their particular type of adoration and fired them for their incompetence. Narcissists are socially maladaptive, constantly changing the rules and introducing new variables. Employees of a narcissist never have a clear picture of what is expected of them because the expectations are in a constant state of flux. My co-workers and I refer to the constantly turbulent office environment as "mood of the moment" management.

Narcissists are great actors. A narcissist can appear to be the perfect manager, fooling those he reports to while treating employees more like robots than human beings, setting unrealistic goals and talking down to them. The narcissist uses subtle brainwashing and controlling techniques to keep employees in their subservient place while appearing to others to be a fair, caring, and competent manager. Last year a member of the board of directors, one of the "adoring worshippers", left that position and became an employee. She quit after just six months, disillusioned and disappointed after seeing for herself what this woman is really like as a boss and knowing this narcissist puts on an act for her board of directors. Her ability to connive and manipulate insures that the only people who serve on the board of directors are pliable and naïve adorers.

A narcissist thrives in a position of authority. His subordinates provide a never-ending supply of the awe, fear, admiration, adoration, and obedience that are required. An employee who fails to provide this needed fodder is soon devalued by the narcissistic boss. This also feeds the narcissist's need to show the world how they must handle everything because they can depend on no one. When this woman goes off on tangents complaining that she must handle everything on all nine desks because the employees are so incompetent, several of us comment that she has climbed back up on the cross. One article I read described a narcissistic leader as a monstrously inverted Jesus who believes he is sacrificing his life because no one else can possibly be qualified to do the job.

It is difficult to identify a narcissist. It took me over twelve years to identify the underlying cause of this woman's erratic behavior. Narcissists can be fascinating personalities. Only on close observation does it become apparent that the narcissist is selfish, self-absorbed, defensive, emotionally needy, and willing to step on everyone to achieve their goals. Because of the instability of the situation and the constant high tension and resulting stress, it is not uncommon for employees of narcissistic bosses to develop high blood pressure, anxiety, depression, gastro-intestinal problems, Post Traumatic Stress symptoms, and other maladies. For nearly fourteen years I watched my co-workers develop one or another of these conditions. Narcissists will never admit they have a problem or seek treatment voluntarily, and the behavior seems to get worse over time. I eventually learned to play the game with her to keep the peace until I could remove myself from her emotionally unhealthy workplace environment.

Chapter 4

CODEPENDENCY

When you find yourself obsessed with someone, walking on eggshells to keep someone you care about from leaving, or trying to figure out how to keep someone safe from themselves, you may be experiencing signs of codependency. Codependency is an uneasy kind of love where one's own true feelings and needs become secondary to someone else's. It often results in unhappiness, frustration and exhaustion instead of closeness and understanding.

Codependency is often a pattern that develops over time, so it can be hard to see. It is also reinforced by occasional payoffs - both on the conscious and unconscious levels. Conscious payoffs may include feeling needed and useful. And you need not feel alone, even when you are, because that other person is on your mind. Other conscious payoffs may include the experiences of infatuation or drama, which can give rise to feelings of romance or excitement that one might be afraid, would otherwise pass them by.

Unconscious roots of codependency run deeper. Sometimes, people develop codependency as a life-long strategy of handling fear and trauma by focusing on others. In some families, about the only positive attention a child gets is when they are being useful and undemanding. As adults, these people often end up care taking others beyond what is useful to either person. A person who is frequently criticized and judged at any age can become vulnerable to believing that they are not worthy of their own support and attention. These are just a few of codependency's causes.

Ultimately, the worst thing about codependency is that it puts you in the backseat of your own life.

Narcissists Are Codependent, Too

People often distinguish narcissists and codependents as opposites, but surprisingly, though their outward behavior may differ, they share many psychological traits. In fact, narcissists exhibit core codependent symptoms of shame, denial, control, dependency (unconscious), and dysfunctional communication and boundaries, all leading to intimacy problems. One study showed a significant correlation between narcissism and codependency.[i] Although most narcissists can be classified as codependent, but the reverse isn't true - most codependents aren't narcissists. They don't exhibit common traits of exploitation, entitlement, and lack of empathy.

Dependency

Codependency is a disorder of a "lost self." Codependents have lost their connection to their innate self. Instead, their thinking and behavior revolve around a person, substance, or process. Narcissists also suffer from a lack of connection to their true self. In its place, they're identified with their ideal self. Their inner deprivation and lack connection to their real self makes them dependent on others for validation. Consequently, like other codependents, their self-image, thinking, and behavior are other-oriented in order to stabilize and validate their self-esteem and fragile ego.

Ironically, despite declared high self-regard, narcissists crave recognition from others and have an insatiable need to be admired - to get their "narcissistic supply." This makes them as dependent on recognition from others as an addict is on their addiction.

Shame

Shame is at the core of codependency and addiction. It stems from growing up in a dysfunctional family. Narcissists' inflated self-opinion is commonly mistaken for self-love. However, exaggerated self-flattery and arrogance merely assuage unconscious,

Internalized shame that is common among codependents.

Children develop different ways of coping with the anxiety, insecurity, and hostility that they experience growing up in dysfunctional families. Internalized shame can result despite parents' good intentions and lack of overt abuse. To feel safe, children adopt coping patterns that give arise to an ideal self. One strategy is to accommodate other people and seek their love, affection, and approval. Another is to seek recognition, mastery, and domination over others. Stereotypical codependents fall into the first category, and narcissists the second. They seek power and control of their environment in order to get their needs met. Their pursuit of prestige, superiority, and power help them to avoid feeling inferior, vulnerable, needy, and helpless at all costs.

These ideals are natural human needs; however, for codependents and narcissists they're compulsive and thus neurotic. Additionally, the more a person pursues their ideal self, the further they depart from their real self, which only increases their insecurity, false self, and sense of shame. (For more about these patterns and how shame and codependency co-emerge in childhood, see Conquering Shame and Codependency.)

Denial

Denial is a core symptom of codependency. Codependents are generally in denial of their codependency and often their feelings and many needs. Similarly, narcissists deny feelings, particularly those that express vulnerability. Many won't admit to feelings of inadequacy, even to themselves. They disown and often project onto others feelings that they consider "weak," such as longing, sadness, loneliness, powerlessness, guilt, fear, and variations of them. Anger makes them feel powerful. Rage, arrogance, envy, and contempt are defenses to underlying shame.

Codependents deny their needs, especially emotional needs, which were neglected or shamed growing up. Some codependents act self-sufficient and readily put others needs first. Other codependents are demanding of people to satisfy their needs. Narcissists also deny emotional needs. They won't admit that they're being demanding and needy, because having needs makes them feel dependent and weak. They judge as needy.

Although, narcissists don't usually put the needs of others first, some narcissists are actually people-pleasers and can be very generous. In addition to securing the attachment of those they depend on, often their motive is for recognition or to feel superior or grandiose by virtue of the fact that they're able to aid people they consider inferior. Like other codependents, they may feel exploited by and resentful toward the people they help.

Many narcissists hide behind a facade of self-sufficiency and aloofness when it comes to needs for emotional closeness, support, grieving, nurturing, and intimacy. The quest of power protects them from experiencing the humiliation of feeling weak, sad, afraid, or wanting or needing anyone-ultimately, to avoid rejection and feeling shame. Only the threat of abandonment reveals how dependent they truly are.

Dysfunctional Boundaries

Like other codependents, narcissists have unhealthy boundaries, because theirs weren't respected growing up. They don't experience other people as separate but as extensions of themselves. As a result, they project thoughts and feelings onto others and blame them for their shortcomings and mistakes, all of which they cannot tolerate in themselves. Additionally, lack of boundaries makes them thin-skinned, highly reactive, and defensive, and causes them to take everything personally.

Most codependents share these patterns of blame, reactivity, defensiveness, and taking things personally.

The behavior and degree or direction of feelings might vary, but the underlying process is similar. For example, many codependents react with self-criticism, self-blame, or withdrawal, while others react with aggression and criticism or blame of someone else. Yet, both behaviors are reactions to shame and demonstrate dysfunctional boundaries. (In some cases, confrontation or withdrawal might be an appropriate response, but not if it's a habitual, compulsive reaction.)

Dysfunctional Communication

Like other codependents, narcissists' communication is dysfunctional. They generally lack assertiveness skills. Their communication often consists of criticism, demands, labeling, and other forms of verbal abuse. On the other hand, some narcissists intellectualize, obfuscate, and are indirect. Like other codependents, they find it difficult to identify and clearly state their feelings. Although they may express opinions and take positions more easily than other codependents, they frequently have trouble listening and are dogmatic and inflexible. These are signs of dysfunctional communication that evidence insecurity and lack of respect for the other person.

Control

Like other codependents, narcissists seek control. Control over our environment helps us to feel safe. The greater our anxiety and insecurity, the greater is our need for control. When we're dependent on others for our security, happiness, and self-worth, what people think, say, and do become paramount to our sense of well-being and even safety. We'll try to control them directly or indirectly with people-pleasing, lies, or manipulation. If we're frightened or ashamed of our feelings, such as anger or grief, then we attempt to control our feelings. Other people's anger or grief will upset us, so that they must be avoided or controlled, too.

Intimacy

Finally, the combination of all these patterns makes intimacy challenging for narcissists and codependents, alike. Relationships can't thrive without clear boundaries that afford partners freedom and respect.

They require that we're autonomous, have assertive communication skills, and self-esteem.

Chapter 5
TRAUMA BONDING

A trauma bond is characterized by betrayal that is so purposeful and self-serving it moves to the realm of trauma. Trauma bonds create chains of trust that link a person to someone who is exploitive, dangerous, abusive and or toxic. A person in a trauma bond feels very confused about their relationship, yet they are unable to break free from it.

Feeling attached to a narcissist or sociopath despite being treated badly is a constant source of anxiety for those recovering from toxic relationships. Victims would like to know why I can't just let this guy go? Why can't I get on with it? Why am I without closure obsessed? Why am I so connected to someone that doesn't feel connected to me? One logical answer to this is that we are normal and that they are not and that normal people want to fix things that are broken in order to get them to work again.

The problem, of course, is that it is not possible to fix a narcissist because he was never right to start with. The narcissist is in essence not really broken at all. He's just what he's and he's not good. That being true, what are we going to do after a Discard when we can't shake the feeling of being just 1/2 a person without him... of feeling utterly attached even when we're separated and even when he's with someone else? Why can't we get rid of the Bad Man? Well, for those seeking a deeper psychological reason for the suffering, there's a response to this and it's a condition often called trauma bonding.

Typically, when we think of trauma bonding, we associate it with The Stockholm Syndrome (TSS), a condition named after a real-life situation where a group of hostages became emotionally attached to their kidnapers. TSS, though certainly similar to trauma bonding, typically occurs in life-threatening situations where the victim is literally afraid of dying from her toxic, abusive partner's hands. Bonding with trauma is more descriptive of the dilemma of attachment that arises from the type of trauma that has caused our emotions (i.e., betrayal and neglect, over and over). It's the type of bonding that can easily occur via passive-aggressive manipulation (i.e. sex, lies, silent treatments) and other forms of narcissistic control.

The narcissist partner understands the process of streamlining the codependency of a victim to the point of least resistance, as cunning as he or she is. In fact, without a single day of formal training, he has figured out that the best way to ensure narcissistic supply is to create trauma bonds with his goals through the "seduce and discard" method. He has come up with an easy way to turn us into the enabler of a narcissist.

The conditioning that leads to trauma bonding focuses on two powerful, repeatedly recurring sources of reinforcement in succession and at perfectly timed intervals. Psychologists call this reinforcement the' arousal-jag' that actually refers to the excitement before the trauma (arousal) and subsequently the peace of surrender (jag). Take a second to think about the behaviors of the narcissist. It's what he's done his whole life to create trauma bonds!

The reinforcement of' Arousal-jag' is about giving a little and then taking it away in well-timed intervals over and over again. Narcissists do this all the time (disappearing / reappearing, silence / chaos) creating an illusion of twisted excitement that strengthens our traumatic bond with them. And to be clear, here the narcissist feels a connection, just as his connection is with the excitement alone and not with us. That's why a narcissist always has multiple partners because his excitement factor doubles and triples. The fact that we are so attached to the chaos as his victims that we are eagerly awaiting a hoover is an added bonus!

During the devalue stage, the excitement before the trauma (of betrayal and neglect) is created... that point in time right before a discard when our intuition has already told us that he will leave based on his behaviors. It's that knot-in - the-stomach feeling, the overwhelming urge to 100 times call his phone, the cognitive dissonance torment.... It's the hours spent scouring the internet in search of clues... it's the feeling we get from the chaos created by the narcissist ALWAYS right before the silence. Like it or not, we get highly addicted to his narcissistic behaviors and all the nonsense that goes with it... and when it's gone, we miss it like a motherfucker... when the narcissist suddenly goes silent. As manipulated and manufactured as it is, we long for the connection until we can barely breathe. Then, just before we either kill ourselves or come to our senses, the narcissist again swoops—like a rising Phoenix—to give us the second reinforcement: the peace of surrender that follows. His reappearance is meticulously timed for maximum effect and usually follows a silent treatment that lasted only one tad longer than the previous one. The narcissist conditioned us to accept less and less so that each time he disappeared, he could get away with more.

If we look back on or inward on our relationship (if we are still in it), we see that the trauma bonding started at the moment the Idolize Phase ends. Maybe we didn't even know that, but you can be sure the narcissist did. As time went by and the narcissistic partner became more successful in managing our relationship expectations, our connection with the nonsense started to stick like super glue. But now that we know it.... that there is a name to hold this bizarre person over us... we can make sure that it never happens to us again. If we're still in the relationship, we can get out (and quickly!) because, unlike a hostage victim who trauma bonds with a kidnapper, we're NOT held at gunpoint and we can escape.

Chapter 6
TOXIC SHAME

When shame becomes toxic, it can ruin our lives. Everyone experiences shame at one time another. It's an emotion with physical symptoms like any other that comes and goes, but when it's severe, it can be extremely painful. Strong feelings of shame stimulate the sympathetic nervous system, causing a fight/flight/freeze reaction. We feel exposed and want to hide or react with rage, while feeling profoundly alienated from others and good parts of us. We may not be able to think or talk clearly and be consumed with self-loathing, which is made worse because we're unable to be rid of ourselves. We all have our own specific triggers or tender points that produce feelings of shame. The intensity of our experience varies, too, depending upon our prior life experiences, cultural beliefs, personality, and the activating event.

Characteristics of Toxic Shame

Unlike ordinary shame, "internalized shame" hangs around and alters our self-image. It's shame that has become "toxic," a term first coined by Sylvan Tomkins in the early 60s in his scholarly examination of human affect. For some people, toxic shame can consume their personality, while for others, it lies beneath their conscious awareness, but can easily be triggered. Toxic shame differs from ordinary shame, which passes in a day or a few hours, in the following respects:

1. It can hide in our unconscious, so that we're unaware that we have shame.
2. When we experience shame, it lasts much longer.
3. The feelings and pain associated with shame are of greater intensity.
4. An external event isn't required to trigger it. Our own thoughts can bring on feelings of shame.
5. It leads to shame spirals that cause depression and feelings of hopelessness and despair.

6. It causes chronic "shame anxiety" - the fear of experiencing shame.

7. it's accompanied by voices, images, or beliefs originating in childhood and is associated with a negative "shame story" about ourselves.

8. We needn't recall the original source of the immediate shame, which usually originated in childhood or a prior trauma.

9. It creates deep feelings of inadequacy.

Shame-Based Beliefs

The fundamental belief underlying shame is that "I'm unlovable - that I'm not worthy of connection. " Usually, internalized shame manifests as one of the following beliefs or a variation thereof:

- ✓ I'm stupid
- ✓ I'm unattractive (especially to a romantic partner)
- ✓ I'm a failure
- ✓ I'm a bad person
- ✓ I'm a fraud or phony
- ✓ I'm selfish
- ✓ I'm not enough (this belief can be applied to numerous areas)
- ✓ I hate myself
- ✓ I don't matter

- ✓ I'm defective, inadequate
- ✓ I shouldn't have been born
- ✓ I'm unlovable

The Cause of Toxic Shame

In most cases, shame becomes internalized or toxic from chronic or intense experiences of shame in childhood. Parents can unintentionally transfer their shame to their children through verbal messages or nonverbal behavior. For an example, a child might feel unloved in reaction to a parent's depression, absence, indifference, or irritability or feel inadequate due to a parent's competitiveness or over-correcting behavior. Children need to feel uniquely loved by both parents. When that connection is breached, such as when a child is scolded harshly, children feel alone and ashamed, unless the parent-child bond of love is soon repaired. However, even if shame has been internalized, it can be surmounted by later positive experiences.

Shameless: Can Toxic Shame Make Someone Shameless?

Although it is possible for an emotion to enhance one's life, it is also possible for an emotion to have the opposite effect. If one feels angry, it could be a sign that they have been violated, but if they always feel this way it shows that something isn't right.

It could mean that one is stuck in the past or that they are in an environment that is not healthy, or both. One is no longer angry during the odd occasion - they are being defined by it.

If one was never angry it would be unhealthy, but to be angry all the time is not the answer either. Their whole life is then being consumed by anger and this is going to affect their ability to experience inner peace and it could end up pushing people away.

However, this is just one example of how an emotion can harm one's life and this can be because they don't allow themselves to experience it or because it has taken control of their life. Emotions are often labeled as being either 'good' or 'bad' and this can cause people to deny how they feel or to be controlled by their feelings.

Information

When one is aware of how they feel, they will be able to use their feelings to guide them. The other option would be for one to ignore how they feel and get caught up in their head. This is not to say that one should let their feelings control them, what it means is that they shouldn't ignore them either.

Just as one has the ability to think for a reason, they also have emotions for a reason. Yet in order for one to be in tune with their emotions and to use the information they are providing, one will need to feel comfortable with their emotions.

Common Approaches

If this isn't the case, one will be used to being controlled by their emotions or they may try to control their emotions. One then ends up feeling overwhelmed or they do all they can to disconnect from how they feel.

While someone could have a pattern of denying how they feel, they could also alternate between the two. How they feel and the environment they are in could play a part in what option they use.

Shame

One of the emotions that one might try to avoid is shame and this is because of the affect it has. Shame can be something that one experience's on the odd occasion or it could be something that defines their whole life.

What this comes down to is the fact that there is healthy shame and toxic shame. Healthy shame will play a part in one having a conscience, toxic shame on the other hand can stop one from having a conscience.

Healthy shame is often said to be something one is born with, whereas toxic shame is usually the result of some kind of abuse. This could have been due to abuse in their adulthood but their childhood is often where it all began.

Healthy Shame

When one is able to experience healthy shame, they won't feel below others and neither will they feel above them - they will simply feel human. This will enable them to stay humble and to respect other people's boundaries. No matter what they achieve, they are still human like everyone else and so there is no reason for them to act 'superior'.

If they were to violate another person's personal space, they might feel guilty and then they would feel ashamed. Healthy shame also allows one to protect their modesty and stop them from being an exhibitionist.

It will also play a vital role in their success - as if one doesn't put in enough effort or go after what they deserve, they will feel 'bad'. Having an interest in other people is another consequence of healthy shame, without it, one can end up being self-absorbed.

The Other Option

These are just a few examples of the role that healthy shame plays in one's life and so when healthy shame has been turned into toxic shame, one can end up being shameless. There is the chance that one will end up feeling inferior and as though they are less-than human.

Here, one is likely to end up being walked over, put up with bad behavior and feel completely worthless. They are flawed and there is nothing they can do about it - this is because toxic shame relates to one's whole being.

Shameless

As a way to avoid feeling this way, one can end up disconnecting from their toxic shame. Through this, one will have a sense of control over how they feel and this could be described as the upside. The down side to this is that one will no longer experience shame and this is going to have a negative impact on their life.

There could still be moments where one ends up being consumed by toxic shame, but this might not take place very often. In today's world, there are many examples of shameless behavior and it could be described as the rule as opposed to the exception. For some people, it will be seen as normal and this could be because they were not around when the world was different.

Consequences

Without the ability to feel shame, one can end up ignoring other people's boundaries and doing things that are not acceptable. They can believe they are superior to other people and that they are perfect. As they are out of touch with their human imperfections, it is then not possible for them to be humble.

One can also talk about them all the time without feeling bad and this means they are not going to be curious about others or have any interest in them. In their mind, they could be the center of the universe and this is therefore going to affect their ability to connect to other people.

This is also going to mean that one won't feel bad for showing certain parts of their body in public and so they won't feel uncomfortable revealing what other people would only reveal behind closed doors. Their body is then another way for them to gain attention and not something that needs to be respected.

Awareness

Shame is something that is not only vital when it comes to one's personal life; it is also an important part of society. As human beings are interdependent, it is essential that people respect each other's personal space and are interested in others, for instance.

If one is out of touch with their shame, it could be a sign that they are carrying toxic shame. This could mean that the emotional experiences of their past have stayed trapped in their body. These will need to be faced and released, and this can take place with the assistance of a therapist or a healer.

Chapter 7
HOW TO IDENTIFY A NARCISSIST

The narcissists' appetite is similar to a leach. The narcissist will suck your blood and energy in order to satiate his own appetite. The narcissists' life source (blood) is: attention, admiration, adoration, and applause. The narcissist dedicates his life in obtaining the above (blood).

The narcissist expects special treatment of some type. He does not believe he should have to wait on line or be placed on hold in an attempt to talk to the "person" he needs to contact. The narcissist believes he should be given special attention from his waitress regardless of how many tables she may be juggling. When he does not receive this attention he becomes filled with anger, disgust, and rage.

I hate to say it, but controlling, narcissistic and self-absorbed people are everywhere. They can be neighbors, classmates, doctors, contractors, teachers, coworkers, bosses, friends and family.

It is an essential skill, one that you will continue to develop throughout your whole life, of recognizing who is harmful to your well-being and removing yourself from their influence.

The narcissist loves to talk about himself and his habits. He loves to hold people hostage discussing his monotonous details about his day. He loves to brag about his daily accomplishments in detail.

The narcissist is sincerely not interested in your life!!

The narcissist may act as if he is interested, however, his actions and behavior are 100% inconsistent with really caring in any way, shape, or form.

The narcissist does not engage in eye contact and does not like to hug and touch people.

The narcissist is offended by anyone who attempts to provide: help, love, assistance, concern, and advice. The narcissist considers this a "slap in his face".

The narcissist will help others, HOWEVER, being helpful is a calculated attempt to receive: adoration, praise, affirmation, encouragement, or to meet a covert desire.

The narcissists' capacity to love and return love was all but extinguished due to his critical, unpredictable, and rejecting mom.

The narcissist is disconnected to emotion and empathy. The narcissist can be thought of as a machine or a zombie.

The primary problem is that narcissists are covert abusers, so they rarely scream, beat you, or trash the house. Instead they will sap your self-worth, remove you from the rest of the world and make you dependent on them.

The key is noticing their behaviors from the actions speak louder than words principle. In every interaction with another person, you should keep close to your heart the feelings they impart to you. This is the narcissist's weakness; they always violate this principle given their behavior and need to manipulate others. They say one thing and do another.

Only About Me, And Never About You, Unless It Has To Do With Me

Seems simple enough, but it manifests itself in subtle ways. Narcissistic people rarely control others in a way that is noticeable to outside eyes, unless those eyes are trained to recognize it.

But here is a simple, foolproof way of figuring out long term if a person has their best interests for you: how much they talk about themselves. With narcissists, everything will be about them, unless something about you helps them reach their ends.

This also comes through as a closed worldview. The narcissist likes what they like and won't like (or downright despise) anything else. They'll keep that hidden for a time, but when it comes down to it, nothing save for them is good or right.

Say Goodbye To Your Connections

So we've established that the narcissist's goal is to control you from within and mess with your mind and perception. How do they do this? By making sure that they are your sole influence.

There's no question that the people around you have immediate and long-term influences on your behavior and psyche. Controlling people realize that and so it is in their best interest to establish themselves as the authority figure, and remove everything else.

The result will be a loss of human contact, along with your identity in the world.

Don't think that just relationships will suffer. Your interests, hobbies and all other activities that the narcissist doesn't benefit from will disappear. It's a slow process, but it's always working and that's why they succeed.

You have priorities for things in your life and narcissists do too. If you love to play the piano, the narcissist will put taking that away on the top of the To-Deprive list.

Something may "accidentally" happen to the piano, but most likely you'll be discouraged to play it. Negative feedback likes "Play something else... ", "Do you practice enough?", "It must be off-key." It will all amount to "Something is wrong with you. Don't do that."

If you're into clothes or fashion, you will never receive a genuine compliment on your tastes. Anything boosts your self-worth takes away from them, and is the enemy. Ad infinitum.

The Emotional Instability Will Affect Other Areas Of Your Life

The loss of motivation, participation, self-confidence, satisfaction and overall happiness will have an adverse effect on your health. Lack of sleep, poor productivity, loss of motivation, illness... something will happen.

It seems a bit ridiculous, but years of emotional abuse, especially from malignant narcissists, will eventually take their toll. If you're raising a family, those traits will be picked up by the children and continue down the family line.

This is why the most important thing is recognition. Getting away from the abuser can be hard, but the hardest part is actually considering that they may be narcissistic and accepting it once you've found the evidence to convince yourself. Then you must take action.

Chapter 8

GREAT SIGNS YOU'RE WITH A NARCISSISTIC

Everyone writes in such great depth about narcissists, and go to great lengths to explain their behavior, but no one ever talks about their enablers; the ones who facilitate the abusers, the ones behind them who unwittingly support it and allow it to continue.

These are their other half, so to speak, and are just as responsible as the narcissist, at least for their negligence. They don't willingly choose to be abused by them, yet they support it and do nothing about it to protect others or themselves.

And no other type of enabler is more facilitating and integral to the abuse, and so can do more to stop it by opposing it, than victims of narcissists. This is because narcissists are so demanding, high-maintenance and ruthless in getting their needs met right now. They rely so heavily upon their enablers and their support to function. Or perhaps more accurately, the ones the abusers abuse and take the brunt of abuse.

I'm willing to be that more people fall into this category than the former, and if we were to properly focus and deal with this problem for assertively, there would be far fewer people putting up with and enabling narcissistic behavior, perpetuating it and allowing it to continue.

Abuse hurts abusers and enablers, but so does enabling. I'm willing to bet it does more harm than abuse simply because it allows and encourages the abuse to continue, thereby creating more abuse in the world. It is a source of encouragement.

If you know or are voluntarily involved with a narcissist in any way, you must be an enabler. Let's find out if you are.

1. **You're expected to Over** - Accommodate and Sacrifice for them, but get nothing in Return and are Never Appreciated for It

You put the needs of others before your own, at your expense. You also hurt the people who actually need you by putting the narcissist's needs before theirs.

Another way of saying this is that you do nothing for yourself because you're always accommodating someone else. You're too busy meeting someone else's needs (read it, demands) to meet your own or even take care of someone who depends solely upon you, like children.

It also means you're preoccupied with others' affairs to the neglect of your own, or to even ignore your own detriments in the service of another. You feel helpless in your ability to admit and then identify your real problems, like the abuse, much less solve them yourself.

The narcissists resists persistently, eternally and ruthlessly. They'll do anything to make sure you can't stop what they're doing and they don't have to change. The whole thing is just running away, it's a race, and they've got to stay ahead of you at every turn. That's all they care about.

They're just running away, running off far and wide to somewhere else in all of the ways they can because they just can't handle it. We don't know what they're feeling, what do we know? But I sure do know that it's not our job to stick around and feel the pain, and spread it around, magnifying and worsening through your enabling.

Another sign is you being over-accommodating and giving in to their demands, no matter how much it costs you personally or comes at your expense.

You'll tell yourself you're being a good person by doing what they ask, when they ask and continue to put up with them, and convince yourself as much.

When they become abusive, you'll tell yourself that they mean well but don't know how to express themselves carefully. In other words, you'll put the abuse in endearing terms, because it's what you need to believe to excuse having to do anything about it.

Truth be told, and you already know this so you can guess what I'm about to tell you, is that you're actually helping them by supporting their fantasy and running yourself ragged and spreading yourself thin.

You're their accomplice and complicit in the abuse. Now don't get me wrong, you don't feel that way. They make you think you're a champ for putting up with them and making it right, doing whatever you have to do to help and protect everyone by sacrificing yourself and putting their needs before your own.

What you're really do in reality is supporting a dysfunctional cycle and regressing pattern of behavior that all depends on whatever mood they happen to be in.

They're making you a chump because you fail to realize that their issues and problems are just ruses to get you into a position of pain and agony so you'll scramble to correct it while they sit on their throne, wait and complain when you do a bad job.

They convince you they're good for you and that's why you stay. But they really do no good at all, and actively seek to harm and continue to do so, like a parasite, until you die and they have to find someone else. That sounds really dramatic, but it's true; they're setting themselves up for life by having someone else burden their problems.

Since we can't avoid being judged and everyone seems to have an opinion about you that they just must share with someone else these days, you're bound to come across what someone else thinks of you and not like it.

The enabler is crippled with fear of being judged by others and seeks to right their wrong and apologize to the person even if they're the ones in fact in the right, which is likely since enablers do very little in the way of deliberately hurting other people, just negligence and convenient denial.

You'll be too focused and concerned with others' needs, especially when they're artificial and designed to get your attention away from something and funnel it onto them; manipulation and dependence, learned helplessness.

How do you tell if that's what they're doing for sure? It's always the same thing and never changes, because they never change.

They never improve themselves and so never improve their problems. They're always stuck in the same place, at the same time and in the same mindset. You never find functional ways of handling them because they aren't functional, they're dysfunctional.

2. **Codependence** - You Both Support and Complement the Each Other's Dysfunctional Behavior Through Your own Dysfunctional Behavior

From being unable to do anything yourself to needing their permission to do anything, and their approval that you did it "right" (which you never will), dependence runs the entire gambit from having to be in constant communication with each other to having to take over and make decisions for each other. It goes both ways.

Now that last part may seem strange, isn't one person dependent and the other independent? One is indeed more independent than the other, and that's you. You're not the one creating the illusion and you're not the one trying to control everything.

Just what is control? What is control and power over someone else's life? Running and controlling your life, it's an illusion, and the purpose of that illusion is to deny their dependence on you. They're with you because you need them, not the other way around. But that's all a ruse to hide their own dependence and project their problems onto you.

Now it seems strange that they don't seem to be or act like they're forcing you into a situation, doesn't it? They technically aren't forcing you to, right? Technically yes, but for a practical matter no.

If you knew what they were doing and experience it for what it really is, what they're thinking and how they regard it, you would regard it as force too. Keep in mind that they always know this too. They know what's good and right or they wouldn't be so good at being bad. They just don't care, or even worse, like to be bad, malevolent and hurt others.

They don't "CONTROL!!!" per say, they "control... " by steering, guiding and directing your behavior, and especially obstructing you are your favorite things to do, because it weakens you. But mostly, they'll gauge their actions so that they produce a specific decision, anticipated and planned response they want from you.

Dependence also comes with denial, rationalizations and excuses for how dependent you really are. You'll naturally come up with these to tell yourself you're in a good place.

3. **Negative Relations** - You Relate to Others by Hate and Conflict and as a Result you Feel bad and Don't Know Why

This one is hard to spot without others' input.

When you find yourself drawing big lines between you and other people you like for minor reasons, you polarize yourself from other people, and become a less attractive person yourself.

Losing touch with family and friends is a high goal of the narcissist, it's required for them to become the only source of input, your bridge to reality, or their reality, which isn't very much like reality at all.

With narcissists, everything is already figured out for you: it's bad. Black and white thinking, negative bias, negative relations to others and the outside world, which you'll also feel increasingly insulated, distanced and removed from.

You have a fear of success and getting what you deserve. Personal or financial success is your empowerment means they lose control of you, and so this means they reward you for being idle and not doing anything at all, it's what makes them feel the most safe, secure and in control of you. They can't control themselves, so they compensate and make up for it by controlling you.

No real actionable steps are taken or progress made towards their spoken goals. Nothing ever happens, nothing ever changes. There's much talk about doing things, but nothing ever comes of it. That's because they like it just how it is right now.

They only entice you and themselves with the prospect of change, but they're too scared to change and they don't really want to anyway. They like eternal parent-child relationship that you two have, which brings me to the next sign: it switches between who is the parent and who is the child all of the time. They'll usually want to be the authority figure you answer to, but when they're scared, they need you to tell them what to do, or else they can't function. That's dependence.

You'll feel bad but you won't know exactly why. I'd practically guarantee with almost 90% certainty that you're with a narcissist if this is the case. There just aren't other personality disorders that are able to do this without you knowing, otherwise you will know and notice it, or at the very least suspect it.

Let me ask you something: have they've ever complemented or openly supported you? How do they talk about you to other people? Is it positive? What do they like and admire about you? What would you and then they say are you're greatest skills? Do you know their answer to any one of these question for sure?

That's because you'll never know, they don't tell you and they don't respect you. They don't even like you. They project every enemy they've ever had, anyone that's ever done wrong to them onto you because they couldn't overcome what that person did to them, so they hate, and they hate and they fume, and they vent with their socially "legitimate" ways, though they aren't at all and are totally unacceptable, yet you still put up with them.

They don't like you, and it's a good bet that you're used to someone disliking you because you're putting up with it right now, so this probably isn't your first, second or even last time being in this situation.

If you feel something's wrong, it probably is. The reason it becomes weird and feels bad to suspect so is that that narcissists make your feelings taboo and convince you that you shouldn't listen to them.

With narcissists, it's their highest priority to make you feel unsure of yourself, and make you think it's all an accident.

It's no accident, it's on purpose; they gauge their behavior to your own personality to see what affect it has on you, to maximize every effort and make every possible effort to hurt, control, and break you down.

Chapter 9

ARE YOU IN A RELATIONSHIP WITH A NARCISSIST?

If you are in a relationship with a narcissist you're living in hell on earth. A narcissist is someone who constantly belittles you at the drop of a hat. A narcissist makes you feel like a peasant while he is the king of not only his domain but yours. You spend every waking moment catering to their every wish, while all your wishes never come true. A narcissist doesn't care about your wishes, hopes, dreams, feelings, judgment or needs. A narcissist only cares about their own, and so should you or you will be sorry.

You may try to keep the peace, but with a narcissist, peace is impossible. They create standards you can never reach, so you will fail again and again and it is up to them to dish out your punishment. And dish it out they will. Since you are all alone with your thoughts and feelings and are unable to verbalize them or exhibit them, you will feel like a robot and a very lonely robot to boot. How did someone so promising and charming hide the fact that they are a narcissist? How did you not see this coming?

A narcissist is always different in the beginning of a relationship, way different. They come across as prince charming, sweep you off your feet and place you on this pedestal and treat you in a way you thought only happened in fairytales. Once you have fallen under their spell, a narcissist then lets his facade crumble. Not to the outside world though. Just in your personal life. They maintain their image for the entire world to see, but allow you to see what is behind the mask, and it is what nightmares are made of.

A relationship with a narcissist is a one way street. The street leads towards them, and away from you. When you are in a relationship with a narcissist you must constantly cater to them and build and maintain their inflated ego and sense of self. At the expense of your own self-esteem, dignity, and ego. Compassion will rarely be given to you by a narcissist, but they expect and demand it from you.

The term "double standards" is perfect to describe a relationship with a narcissist. It is all about them, and has nothing to do with you. They get the praise, you get the complains and reprimands. They have the say on everything, you are afraid to say anything and better keep your mouth shut. If they are not happy, you will not be allowed to be happy either. A narcissist doesn't care about your happiness; they are only concerned with their own.

Since narcissists are so in love with themselves, they cannot really be capable of really loving you because they can never put you first. Sure, if you try and end things with a narcissist they may go overboard to get you back. But is it really because they love you and will change? No, it is for their own ego, they do not want to be abandoned. THEY can leave YOU, but you cannot leave THEM. So how do you know if you are involved with a narcissist as a friend, lover or family tie?

A narcissist has an over inflated ego and thinks they are above others and look down on everyone else they deem not up to their standards. Because they are special, rules do not apply to them. To everyone else, yes, but to them, no. A narcissist has delusions of grandeur. They are not ordinary so why should they have an ordinary wife, ordinary kids and ordinary job or an ordinary house? That may be good enough for "other people" but not for them. They have a sense of entitlement like no one you have ever met before or since. They think other people are jealous of them or out to get them.

Narcissists feel you should be able to take criticism from them, and they will give it to you constantly. However, you cannot criticize them for ANYTHING. They will also twist your words and take things you say in a critical way when you did not mean it that way. They will have temper tantrums when they are unhappy over any little thing.

Narcissists will keep you guessing. One day they act like all is wonderful and they adore you, the next day, they are as cold as ice and treat you like a stranger or an enemy. A narcissist cannot sympathize or empathize with anyone other than themselves. Other people's feelings, unless it is to get what something from them, are irrelevant.

Trying to Find Closure with a Narcissistic Relationship

It's often difficult to find closure with Narcissists, such as why things need to end. Their emotional capacity is often so impaired, that it is often best to try to find closure on your end. Cutting off cold turkey is so you can begin to heal apart from them. Having a little contact with them will only create opportunities for them to try to convince you not to leave until you give in and the cycle starts again. To allow for even a little contact every so often, is like leaving the door unlocked to your house when you've been alerted that the neighborhood has experienced multiple thefts. People who have either married or had children with a Narcissist or were children of Narcissists will need a lot of emotional support, healing, and very firm boundaries with minimal contact as possible with the Narcissist.

Therapy is often a necessity along with very supportive people for those who were formerly involved with a Narcissist. A support group for victims of Narcissistic abuse might also be another ideal option. Feeling drained, caught in a web of the Narcissist's deceit, the shock of finding out they were not who they originally presented can cause a lot of trauma emotionally and psychologically. They saw Dr. Jeckl and Mr./Ms. Hyde up close and personal. Loose associations to the Narcissists may find it very hard to believe the Narcissist is this way because they only see the fascade of who they are. It's only those who get entangled closely to them. In this case, I'm referring to a boyfriend/girlfriend, or wife and husband.

The Narcissistic Reaction and Process throughout the Relationship

Narcissistic Injury and Narcissist Rage Occurs during the Devaluing Stage. They cannot tolerate to hear criticism of negative feedback about themselves. To do so, is what's called a Narcissist Injury (NI). A healthy person can take constructive feedback well, and doesn't let that feedback destroy them. For a relationship to be healthy there must be the safeness to give and take constructive feedback. This is not an ability a Narcissist is capable of. To a Narcissist, a NI can often feel like you've thrown a grenade into their lap. They want you to see them as perfect, like in the beginning of the relationship where 'love is blind.' They can do no wrong, and they want you to embody that too. They don't want to see cracks and flaws in their reflections you mirror to them. Of course, this is impossible for any human being walking on this earth. This is what is idealized in the mind of a Narcissist. When a Narcissist's ideal is shattered, they begin to devalue and abuse the one they are in a relationship with. (e.g. sharing your needs, problems you might have in the relationship, constructive feedback, wanting to establish firmer boundaries can evoke their abuse)

The original myth of Narcussus, the nymph who fell in love with his own reflection is where the term Narcissist originated. He couldn't take his eyes off himself or tear himself away from the reflection that he died there at last. You start to see that they have made you be the reflection in the water. They started by putting you on a pedestal, then proceeded to knock you down with time because they had the impossible demand to expect perfect mirroring at all times in order to keep their over-inflated, grandiose but fragile ego intact and the false sense of self fortified. (i.e. you adoring them and praising them at all times).

Their ability to feel all levels of emotions, joy, empathy, compassion, sadness, and anger is greatly impaired. They are unable to get in touch with their own feelings that range from joy, delight, anguish, compassion and empathy, without it coming from a warped place that threatens their false self. On some level, many Narcissists may even envy that ability in you. They've had to wear a mask to hide these types of emotions which were often rejected, condemned or belittled by the very people who were supposed to nurture, protect, and help them put words to emotions that they were experiencing during the developmental stage or their life. In order to survive their often difficult childhood years, they've had to push away the vulnerable parts of themselves and keep it safe in hiding.

On the flip side of the coin, they are also terrified to be engulfed by your needs in a relationship. In order to tolerate this, they start to pull away from you. It might look like they create the distance through abuse. To see these vulnerable areas you are able to accept and acknowledge in yourself is a threat. They are unable to successfully access those vulnerable emotions within themselves, and literally have a fracture in their soul. (i.e. mind, will and emotions that created the false self. Their real self has not been able to develop properly.) They abuse their victims, and can often have self-destructive behaviors through suicidal ideations, addictions, substance abuse, and high-risk taking behaviors. (This is not for every case, but can be common problem among Narcissists.)

When you've talked to the Narcissist about what your needs are, or what is starting to bother you it's very likely you would have incurred in them what's called, Narcissistic Rage. This is because you implied to them (in their mind) that they are not perfect, and that you are not perfect. They find your range of emotions an engulfing threat, so distance themselves further from you, and thus come the Narcissistic Rage. This is one of the means they distance, devalue then discard.

Their sense of self is already fragile so to defend against experiencing any vulnerable emotions that you are capable of, they often want to retaliate against you. The retaliation can be ruthless and feel cold-hearted should you inadvertently incur their wrath. They will stonewall anyone that threatens to damask the perfect false self-image.

This is where the "love interest" of a Narcissist feels devalued and drained. The devaluing and draining process gets stronger over time as long as you choose to stay connected to the Narcissist. A Narcissist cannot meet the emotional needs of others, and certainly not for the one they are in a relationship with. Your emotional and relational needs goes into a deficit the longer you stay in a relationship with a Narcissist. Because vulnerable emotions are threatening to engulf the Narcissist, many often have or currently have addictive behaviors and addictions to substances.

The Discarding Phase in a Narcissistic Relationship

During the devaluing stage, Narcissistic individuals also shift into the discarding stage. Discarding can come in the form of: disappearing for periods at a time. It can range from days to months and show up out of the blue without warning. They can talk about being bored in general with their life or with their victims. They were often involved in multiple relationships to cultivate more supply with no sense of remorse about how it affects their victims. (That's often the primary reason they dropped out of your radar for a period of time.)

When those supplies run low, they pop back into your life. If victims try to reject and not allow the Narcissist to return, the begging and promising to change behavior comes out. Often times, the behavior is more lies and deceit. For example, a married man with children met the victim and lied. He told the victim he was single, and started a hot and heavy relationship with them. As the devastating truth came out, the victim is shattered. They promise they are planning to leave their wife and file for divorce. The victim is promised many things, but is nothing more than false hope and lies. Victims often struggle to break the connection to the Narcissist; this is why a lot of support and sound therapy is needed.

Some Types of Psychological Abuse Narcissists Use

This is not a complete list of all the types of abuse, but is the common ones I am bringing to light. Other personality disorders may also share similar characteristics of psychological abuse as Narcissists listed below.

1. **Gaslighting**: this is a term that was coined after the 1944 movie called, 'Gaslight,' with Ingrid Bergman. It's designed to make the victim doubt themselves through second guessing, it disorients, confuses the victim. They are often left feeling invalidated through the Narcissist's denial. When a victim is trying to distance or cut off the Narcissist, it's good to be aware of the 2-faced nature of the Narcissist. They become abusive to those they are more "deeply involved" with such as a significant relationship, in a marriage, family members. Initially, they were very charming to you. To everyone else, they are charming and delightful. It's wise to be careful who you share with the issues you are having with your Narcissistic relationship. Others

who don't realize what's going on can say comments of disbelief and if you are not prepared, it can invalidate the feelings you are experiencing. It can make you feel like you are going crazy. That's because the disbelief comes from only seeing the charming mask, and not the nightmare unveiled behind the mask.

2. **Blame Shifting**: Narcissist are unable to own up to failures, imperfections and even constructive feedback. They often retaliate with any "complaints" brought up against them through gaslighting and then blame shifting to protect their grandiose false self.

3. **Triangulating**: this is where a third party is brought into the middle of the discussion. The third party might not even be physically present. It's used to create distance and power over and from the victim. For example, a "Narcissistic player" starts another "relationship" with another person and intentionally brings them up to the victim to wound them and gain the upper hand. They might bring them up to you then threaten to abandon you.

4. **Manipulation/Exploitation**: This comes in many forms, but its primary purpose is to control the victim and to feel empowered. (e.g. they access supply

through often making their victims miserable.) A Narcissistic player might gain internal power and euphoria when they see they can make you miserable by manipulating your emotions through game playing. This adds to their magical thinking of being all powerful.

5. **Bullying**: This is also about control and a type of manipulation. When their rage is triggered, a Narcissist will often bully victims through accusations from a distorted sense of reality, (e.g. accusing the victim of cheating on him/her, but they are also cheating on the victim. In their eyes, they justify their behaviors.)

6. **Hot and Cold Bombing then Withdrawals**. When they are hot and cold, they are extremely hypersensitive. In their Narcissistic Rage they have an excessively explosive temper pillaging you in the process with abuse. When they are trying to win you in the beginning, or win you back from cutting them out of the victim's life, the charm, seduction and sweet talking manifest. They might overwhelm you with 30-40 texts a day, or call you multiple times in a day. When they discard you, or devalue you, they push you away coldly or disappear.

7. **Denial**. In the beginning, when you start to notice "something's wrong" in the relationship you might try to bring up things that are nagging at you about the Narcissist and the relationship. They might begin by denying the issue. As it progressing, it worsens into gaslighting.

8. **One-Up on You**. Narcissists are unable to neither have a normal relationship of equality nor compliment one to another. They often struggle with jealousy and often believe others are jealous of them. Many are very competitive and try to gain one notch up on you by knocking you down. It could be subtle and seemingly benign, or obvious attack on your sense of self or accomplishments. They are unable to be happy for your success or accomplishments in your life. If you had a great relationship with your mom, they might brag about the great relationship with their mom at the point of lying to avoid feelings of shame. They might put you down in that scenario in order to cast out their feelings of shame and pin it on their victims. (Called projection)

9. **Destructive Acting Out Behaviors**: Narcissists are like 2 year old children in an adult body. They will throw tantrums or sulks. They will often use emotional

blackmail that is fear based. It include guilt trips or tacking their internalized feelings of shame onto you. Keeping vigilant track of your whereabouts or all your movements.

10. **Everything becomes a competition in which they MUST always WIN**! In an argument, there's no healthy coming to terms with agreeing to disagree. They must be right, better, smarter, richer, more attractive and believe everyone wants to be like them. This can become very personal to them. Narcissists will often compete against you rather than relate with you. They pit others against you as well; so if you are dating the narcissist, they start to make comparisons with you and "the competition" undermining you and any shred of secure feelings in the relationship. They may even seem delighted when they see any dismay or pain your face. That's exactly what gives them the Narcissistic Supply. It does nothing but make you feel bad, worthless, and less valued in their eyes.

The Aftermath Of A Relationship With A Narcissist; I Gathered Real Live Occurrence Shared Stories From An Expert.

Andra asked me for help with the aftermath of her relationship:

"I ended a relationship a month ago that was short but intense. I was shocked by his reaction and what he has subsequently done, and I happened to find that article you wrote about NPD (Narcissistic Personality Disorder), and to my dismay all but one of your listings describe him and us almost exactly. I have tried to get over it by telling myself that the relationship wasn't sustainable anyway and better that I got out of involvement with an NPD, but I still feel hurt and in pain about it that leaves me unable to focus on the things I need to do in my own life - basically abandoning myself. I have tried to do Inner Bonding, but not been able to alleviate the hurt, and additionally the shame I feel about being so taken advantage of by what he's done with my belongings. I'd be grateful for any helpful advice and suggestions."

First, Andra needs to move into compassion for herself rather than shaming herself. She needs to accept that, as I stated above, many people are vulnerable to narcissists due to not giving to themselves the love and valuing that they need. Due to their own self abandonment, they are vulnerable to narcissistic charm, and rather than judging herself for it, Andra needs to learn from it. She needs to discover why she was vulnerable to the narcissist. When she learns to give herself the love she needs, she will be able to focus on her own life.

Andra is dealing with problems regarding her belongings, which is difficult, but sometimes people who have been married to a narcissist also find themselves going through intense emotional and financial trauma. The aftermath of a marriage with a narcissist can be one of the worst experiences of your life, so it's very important to do the inner work necessary to no longer be vulnerable to the charms of a narcissist.

Ronda asked:

"At the beginning of this year I ended a very intense and also dysfunctional relationship, and later found out that my ex was a typical narcissist. I've had a lot of learning and healing... but I still have my ex on my mind a lot... Why do I keep recalling him? What can I do to complete my healing?"

What Ronda is experiencing is the result of the intensity of the connection that can occur with a narcissist. She likely fell in love with his soul, but then could not tolerate his narcissistic wounded self. She misses the fun and connection she had with him, and she likely thinks of him when she is feeling lonely. Ronda needs to be compassionate with her when she is lonely, and make it okay to miss the intensity and the connection, and learn to give herself the experience of meaningful connection, with Spirit or with others, in a healthy way.

Stuart asked me in a session:

"I know leaving the relationship was the right thing to do. I now see that she is a narcissist. Most of the time, I feel great about my new life. But there are times I feel heartbroken even though I know the relationship was not good for me. I'm wondering why?"

Like Ronda, Stuart fell in love with the essence of his former partner. He loved the love, attention and passionate sex she gave him, and he ignored the red flags that showed up along the way. He is heartbroken because he misses her essence, but he could not tolerate her wounded self. His partner turned out to be a major liar and extremely manipulative. She hurt him deeply, but that doesn't mean that he isn't heartbroken at losing the wonderful parts of the relationship. Like everyone who ends up in a relationship with a narcissist, Stuart needs to heal his own wounded self who is vulnerable to the kind of attention and passion that narcissists often offer. He needs to learn to give the love and attention to himself that he seeks from others. He needs to learn to stop abandoning himself.

If you are susceptible to the charms of the narcissist, then you need to explore the self-abandonment that is the underlying cause of this vulnerability. The more you learn to love yourself, the more you become tuned into the manipulative energy of the narcissist. Energetically, there is a big difference between the 'love' the narcissist offers and the love offered by a genuinely loving person. There are many red flags along the way, which become apparent to you when you are connected with your feelings and your spiritual guidance.

Chapter 10
WHY WE FALL FOR NARCISSISTS

I've always known about narcissists, in different contexts I've been heading the term. However, after a close encounter with one of them a couple of years ago, I started to pay close attention to it and research it. I knew this person for decades, but I never realized they fit the category of narcissistic. It wasn't until I rationalized the red flags and looked deep into the message that my instinct had for me that I realized who I was actually dealing with. It was an aha moment for me to identify and validate my intuition. I've always been curious about them since that time. I began to notice how present they are around us in different relationships while learning about narcissism. A parent, a boss, a partner, a best friend, an in - law, a member of the family, for example.

Most of us will be reflecting on or recovering from a romantic run-in with a narcissist at one point or another. Whether it was a short or long-term connection, it's likely that during the post-mortem relationship, you'll wonder how you got sucked in by his charms, how you missed all the warning signs, what made you so vulnerable to the charms of a cold-hearted manipulator (and often a cheat). It is usually not much comfort to realize that after her encounter with the original Greek myth Narcissus, these are probably the same questions that the hapless nymph Echo asked herself.

Why is it so stress-free to be seduced by a narcissist?

The short answer: nothing the narcissist says or does is what it looks like, and he or she is very, very manipulative — and very attractive and engaging, at least at the beginning of things.

The longer response is based on research into how narcissists work in relationships. Below are 5 lessons science learned about narcissists. The findings are both cautionary and revelatory.

<u>Take into consideration</u>:

The Very Abilities That Brand Someone A Narcissist Account For His Or Her First Appeal

Probably you should remember that old lesson at this point: don't judge a book by its cover. Narcissists exude self-confidence— it's grandiosity fed by a heartfelt sense of entitlement — and they're going to do whatever they can to snow you so you're the admirer they need. Researcher Mitja Back and colleagues conducted studies to determine why such a great first impression is made by a narcissist. Self-representation is one reason. Because narcissists are all about validating themselves, they are focused on presentation, including clothing, grooming, and accessories. (My own narcissist was driving a Porsche and wearing very expensive clothes.) Some of them are born attractive physically, but they all work to maintain a polished and appealing look. Self-presentation also draws positive attention to itself— whether through a dramatic or commanding style, wowing you humorously, or captivating you with sparkling conversation, an easy smile, and beautiful manners— because a narcissist needs a thriving audience.

And that's what the studies showed exactly. Researchers had each stand up and introduce themselves to the group after administering a Narcissistic Personality Inventory in one study of 72 college freshman— all of whom met for the first time and thus strangers to each other. Then each person was evaluated in terms of looks, stylishness, attitude, and popularity by the others. The latter was assessed by asking if the person was pleasant and if the observer wanted to know the person.

Would you be surprised to learn that the most appealing and charming were the narcissists? Many of us would find ourselves squirming and anxious as we introduced ourselves to a room filled with strangers but not the narcissist, who, as the researchers put it, is "socially bold." A second experiment showed another group a video of self-presentation from the first study and, once again, the narcissist scored big on popularity.

So, if it makes you feel stupid to fall for a narcissist, appreciate the fact that you have a lot of business.

Confidence and that sense of entitlement make the narcissist look sexy and seem to be a worthy potential mate.

That's what was found in a series of experiments by Michael Durfner and others, the last of which is positive evidence. They actually sent male participants to a German city's streets to approach 25 women—random strangers— and get their phone numbers, email addresses, and other contact information. Research assistants followed the men and interviewed the women they had approached, asking if they had enjoyed the contact and chat, if they liked the man, and if they had been attracted to him. Of course, the more narcissistic the man was, the more he made contacts, and the more attractive he appeared to women.

The narcissist knows how to do it easily. Unfortunately, while the performance seems to be directed at the person with whom he or she is, it really isn't. It's all about self - validation. However, it takes time for the partner of the narcissist to figure this out.

The Narcissist Is Expert At Playing Games

Studies show that narcissists need relationships but prefer short-term ones without commitment. They tend to scout for the next connection that suits their needs while they're still in a relationship so it's highly possible that they will cheat on their current romantic interest. One reason narcissists can cause a lot of emotional damage to their partner is all the mixed signals: the narcissist wants to be in a relationship—but only on its terms. Their style of relationship, like W's work. Keith Campbell and others showed that game-playing is one that gives them control over the relationship and their partner. They love power and guard their autonomy — levitating real intimacy and engagement — but they want your attention and sexual satisfaction. It's like being in a mirror house, except the one the narcissist holds in his or her hand is the only mirror that matters.

Campbell and his colleagues at the end of their paper address the question of why a narcissist would be dated by anyone. They also observe that, given the charm and charisma of the narcissist, it takes time to make his tactics wise. They also venture that narcissists may target individuals who are low in self-esteem — on the surface, after all, narcissists look like big catches— and who are prone to self-doubt.

Alas, it's a simple truth that it's the sincere person who is likely to get hurt when a sincere person gets tangled up with someone who plays games.

On A Practical Level, The Narcissist May Be Good In Bed

James K. McNulty's and Laura Widman's work focused specifically on how narcissism works in the sexual domain— because, as they write, "Having a quality sexual relationship is an integral part of having a quality romantic relationship." Interestingly, narcissists are a very mixed bag, sexually. For their partners, they lack empathy, but research shows that empathy is part of a good sexual experience. Open communication is also part of good sex, but open communication does not interest the self-focused narcissist. They also note that narcissists tend to be sexually aggressive and prefer infidelity — traits that are inimical to a good sexual relationship.

But here's where the narcissist's seductive power comes in, along with the emotional confusion that he or she can shower on your life: narcissists like sex, and they're very focused on how good they're at all — including sexual abilities. So it matters a lot to them to be "good in bed." In the sexual domain, entitlement, exploitation, and an inflated sense of skill are the narcissistic traits that are activated. Studies by McNulty and Widman on marital satisfaction confirmed all these narcissistic observations — both the communication and intimacy negatives and the sexual skill - related positive ones.

However, a second study by these authors revealed that predicting infidelity was sexual narcissism, not general narcissism. It is estimated that 25% of married men and 20% of married women cheat—so all cheaters are obviously not narcissists. McNulty and Widman found that the partner was associated with infidelity with a sense of sexual entitlement, pride in sexual abilities, and a lack of sexual empathy.

The Narcissist Doesn't Forgives Or Forgets

There is another reason why a relationship with a narcissist will be rocky: According to the work of Julie Juola Exline and others, conflict resolution with narcissists is almost impossible because, on the one hand, they are skeptical about the value of forgiveness and, on the other, easily offended. They tend to carry out a cost-benefit analysis when in a relationship there has been a transgression of any kind and generally do not see the benefit of either forgiving or forgetting. They're fast holding a grudge.

There is a bit of good news in that it may be the light you need to see the spots of the leopard for those of you unlucky enough to fall for a narcissist: that grudge - holding attitude and the behavior that accompanies it.

Chapter 11
HOW NARCISSISTS CONTROL YOU IN 3 STEPS

I'm going to show you the exact method narcissist's use to manipulate your perceptions so they can vent onto you and meet their needs and bear their bad feelings. Narcissists are complicated, but they're also formulaic and have noticeable patterns of behavior when you're taught how to spot them.

Narcissists have unresolved personal problems they're forced to deal with on a regular, continual basis. When this bombardment of bad feelings hits, their method for relieving the pain is to emotionally abuse others into accepting it as their own. All

Narcissists employ this method because it does three things for them:

It immediately takes it off of them. They feel it's your problem and not theirs. You are the problematic one and they are problem-free. When you feel bad and do poorly, it makes them feel good, especially if they're the ones who made you feel bad.

They feel like a good person in the process, another narcissistic requirement, though the definition of good and social good means different things to different narcissists.

And finally, they enjoy hurting you. They derive pleasure from your pain. It makes them feel powerful and in control over you, which makes them feel good and in control over themselves.

They have an internal need to dump their problems onto you, but they can't appear malicious while doing it or they'd have nothing to start with.

They need to be your "friend" to capitalize on the opportunity to "help" you with the problem they've just created for you. Narcissists always make sure there are plenty of problems for them to capitalize on. If there isn't a problem, they'll create one.

So the problem is not a problem itself, the problem is they need an outlet right now and they have to create a problem to get one. Here's how they turn nothing into something they can use for years and years against you, building off of it successively.

Here's their procedure:

1. Create a problem that involves you, then spin it so that you're responsible and obligated to fix it

It must involve you because then they can turn it appropriately so that you have to be the one to fix it. Not only does it involve, but you caused it, you're the source of the problem and your behavior needs to be corrected by them. You're responsible and accountable for this particular problem, because it involves something you did, like leave clean clothes in the dryer for too long.

Problem creation is the hard part, so they generally keep a list of things in their heads they can use. This list builds over time, and they're constantly finding and maintaining new angles to bug you.

Spinning is the easy part, because you'll do the work for them with your low self-esteem. They've already chosen and specially selected you as their victim, and that you'll bear the brunt of their abuse. Whereas creating a problem requires proof, putting it all on you is personal and emotional; it requires no reason or logic. They make you feel it is your fault, and being good person, you'll rush in/swoop down to fix it.

The problem is, leaving clean clothes in the dryer is not an adequate excuse and cannot justify the abuse they need to wreak on you, so they must make it much worse than it is or they'll look bad.

What's the problem going to be? Well that all depends on how you conduct yourself and live your life. Narcissists turn positive character traits into character flaws that bother them. No matter what you do, they're going find things wrong with you. They have to take issue with you as a person if you're going to serve as their doormat.

You're exceptional qualities that distinguish you from everyone else are the biggest risk to them. By denigrating those things you hold most dear about yourself they kill two birds with one stone by not only draining your source of strength against them but also turning it into a weapon against you. If you're a human being on the planet earth, they'll find something that is "wrong" with you.

2. Position Themselves as the Victim to the Problem and the Only one who can Possibly Solve It

It's crucial that the distinction be made without saying: you caused the problem and they are the victim of it, which makes you feel like you're in the wrong and the bad guy. Unless you spring into action to remedy it, you did it on purpose and enjoy hurting them.

Now you kick it into high gear and plunge right in attempting to alleviate the problem, but something strange happens: they actually block you from solving the problem, aggressively obstructing and second guessing you.

Why? Because you can't solve the problem, you aren't capable. If you did that you'd be good and redeeming yourself for you abuse of them. They must be the ones to do it, because they're so great. They don't have to solve it because they're not responsible for it, but they will because they're such fantastic people.

3. Now That You're Obligated to Solve it, They'll Undermine you and set you up to Fail

The object here is to make you feel bad, that you weren't enough and you failed them not for lack of effort but because you're inadequate. Please remember that no matter what you do, you will fail, they've seen to that already.

If somehow you manage to overcome their barriers and solve the problem, they must compensate by being less satisfied with your solution. This is even worse because now they have to abuse you a different, more direct way to vent their angst.

Now they just need to steal the spotlight from you, persevere and "solve" the problem themselves. As you've probably guessed, there's no problem-solving. Since they're the ones who created the problem, they're in control can make it go away by not bringing it up again.

It's "solved" because they feel better and they successfully made you the screw-up. The problem has served its true purpose in covering for the real problem and can now vanish into thin air.

They feel better because now they have their release, they don't feel as self-conscious anymore and their self-image is not only intact, but bolstered and without a blemish. Yours however isn't and you're worse off now than before this "problem" arose.

The problem was they felt bad and needed to dump it onto you. They dump it because they can't express it, much less acknowledge it themselves. All they know is that they feel bad and abusing you makes them feel better.

Solving the problem makes things worse for them and for you. They won't get their release, will feel bad and find another way to vent onto you, maybe with the same problem but most likely with a new one.

How Narcissists Use The Silent Treatment To Discipline Their Victims

Narcissistic partners are fond of using the silent treatment and other passive aggressive punishments on anyone who dares to call them out on suspicious or questionable behaviors. Particularly demoralizing, invoking the silent treatment is a narcissist's way of teaching the victim a lesson and asserting control in the relationship. I speak from experience when I say that subjecting someone to a silent treatment is one of - if not the most - hurtful things a narcissist will do to fulfill his relationship agenda. What the silence "says" to the victim is that he or she is not even worth acknowledging... that the victim's very existence isn't worth the narcissist's time of day.

My ex-narcissist boyfriend of twelve-years subjected me to a narcissistic silent treatment about every three to six months in the beginning. Twelve years later, the silence was coming to me on a rotation of two weeks on and two weeks off. Of course, the relationship had become so ridiculous by that point that I would almost welcome the silence as hurtful as it was. Even now, I hate to think about the girl who was suffering at the other end of that rotation because I'm sure she existed.

No matter how long or how often you are subjected to a silent treatment, the feeling you are left with is indescribable. To ramp up the pain, the narcissist, sociopath, or psychopath typically will not even fully elaborate on why he or she is ignoring you. This causes feelings of desperation and often compels the recipient to apologize simply to apologize, hoping to end the nightmare. Of course, everything the victim feels when shunned and ignored is exactly what the narcissist intends that person to feel. Remember, everything a narcissist does or says is a means to an end. Behind every narcissistic action, there is always an evil motive. With the silent treatment, the motive is all about control.

Meanwhile, as the victim suffers, the narcissist goes on about his/her business until, at some point, the punishment becomes "enough". When this happens, the narcissist usually returns unexpectedly offering barely, if any, explanation as to why he was gone or not answering the door, phone, emails, or texts. Having felt so broken and dejected during the silence, a victim is often so relieved that it's over that she demands no answers anyway. This particular response, by the way, is an intended result of this type of passive-aggressive punishment and one of the powerful ways that a person with this personality disorder manages down the expectations of others so that they expect less of him and he gets away with more.

You must understand that there is never a good reason for absolute silence. Communication is key to any relationship and it is not be controlled by just one person. The narcissistic partner will stop at nothing to hurt you and will cross all boundaries - personal and otherwise - to break your spirit and, literally, destroy you. The silent treatment is just one weapon in the narcissistic partner's never-ending arsenal of pain producers and you are the only one who can stop it. Trust me, the narcissist never will.

Chapter 12
HOW THE NARCISSIST USES MIND CONTROL TO BREAK DOWN AND REBUILD YOUR IDENTITY

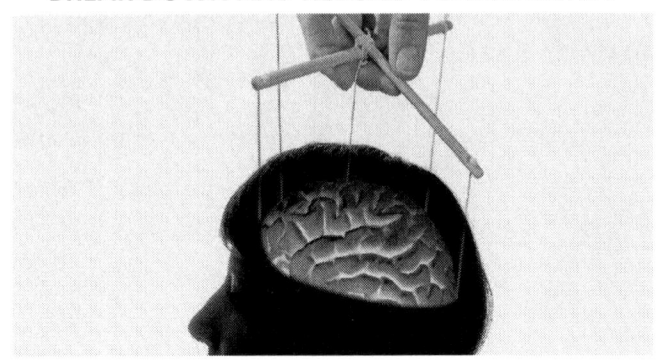

The trick of mind control that differentiates mind control from brainwashing is how the' victim' perceives the manipulator. The manipulator is an evident enemy in brainwashing. Physical strength is often involved. The person may be in a position where the manipulator's wishes depend on their life. The mind control trick is that the victim thinks that the manipulator is a friend, or a teacher, someone at heart with their best interests. This means the person being manipulated is a willing participant, believing that they are being helped and cared for. They believe that they make their own choices. This makes it more dangerous than holding a weapon in the head of someone!

Subtle Control

Narcissists know to how to use subtle control, so you don't even realize you're doing what they want.

Narcissists use trigger phrases to control you. Some common phrases include disappointment and statements about their feelings. They may remind you of how you're supposed to behave and think.

Being your own person is the best way to escape the control of a narcissist. However, those suffering from low confidence may find it difficult to be themselves so that they can escape a narcissist's control.

Signs Of A Narcissist's Mind Control

Some narcissists are good at hiding their real nature. Beware of these signs:

A narcissist who is using mind control doesn't care about your feelings or pain.

They will also use a variety of emotional and other manipulative techniques to get you to do or think a certain way.

Narcissistic people may use flattery and love to affect you. This will be used in turn with aggression and anger to control you. The victim is also isolated from others, so the narcissist can manage him or her easier.

The narcissist will try to create chaos and uncertainty, so the victim doesn't know what to expect and lives in constant fear. This also gives the narcissist more control because they get to decide how things are handled. The victim is left so scared and confused that they can't even escape.

Gaslighting and shifting blame are common techniques used by a narcissist.

How to escape mind control

It's usually not easy to get away from the mind control of a narcissist.

In some cases, the victims need outside intervention and help to get away. You may need to seek help from a trusted family member, friend, or therapist to figure out how to escape. Support is essential.

Avoiding the narcissist physically may not be enough to escape his or her control. Any type of communication, such as phone conversations or even texts, can place you back under their thumb.

It's important to remember that it will take time to recover and heal. Your self-esteem and confidence can be shattered. Your ability to make decisions on your own can be affected. Your identity practically disappears under the narcissist's control and desires.

In some cases, once a person escapes one narcissist, they find another one. This sad pattern can repeat, so it's crucial not to fall into it.

The mind control that a narcissist can perform may astound you. They're capable of convincing you of anything and making you doubt your own memory. They're able to get inside your head with a simple phrase. Take care of yourself by learning how to deal effectively with a narcissist.

The Language Narcissists Use To Control And Traumatize Their Victims

Narcissists are language masters who use words to mislead, coerce, seduce, and mislead. They have a viper's forked tongue and have no doubts about spouting poisonous, vitriolic abuse on their victims. Their preferred method of manipulation is verbal trickery and they have the ability to say the right thing at the right time to confuse, belittle and degrade the other person.

They devalue their victims, intentionally trying to make them feel worthless in order to subjugate them to their will. The narcissist's relentless mind games are unbelievably harmful to those on the receiving end; they can lead to anxiety, depression, and a host of other psychological effects. The bombardment leaves the victims traumatized, with emotional pain that appears to have no end. They get mentally crippled by the assault, failing to understand what is going on or how to escape from it.

That's why educating yourself about the sadistic language of narcissists is so important; only then can you recognize it when you come across it. Knowing their ways will help you shape your shield against their attacks and prepare you for a quick escape if you are ever lured in by one.

If you have been abused by a narcissist before, a better understanding of how they work may help in your recovery process. It may help to convince you that you have been a victim in the whole episode and not just a participant. Whatever role you think you've played, you're likely to only act out the will of the narcissist. So, here are just some of the ways a narcissist takes advantage of language to control his (or her) victim.

Low-level Furtiveness Abuse

This is a paraglider for the almost unceasing stream of small, almost insignificant comments that form the basis of verbal abuse by a narcissist. This is how they usually start exercising control over their victims, starting early in the relationship when their otherwise charming demeanor might seem nothing more than a small flaw.

They often say things like "you're a very sensitive thing aren't you?" with a friendly smile on their face. "Or' no, you misunderstood what I was saying.' These are the beginnings of a much longer process of wearing down the victim, but they are seldom seen for what they are because of their apparent insignificance. This kind of hidden abuse will continue as an accompaniment to further, more insidious attacks throughout a relationship.

The "Exceptional Relationship" Saga

Another thing narcissists will do is to convince their victim of the unique and special bond they have, especially at the beginning of a relationship. They may use phrases like "I have never before felt this kind of love for anyone" or "what I feel for you is so much more than what most people think love is." This is a form of grooming that begins to sow the seeds for the future tolerance of harmful abuse of the victim. They are lulled into a sense that, unlike anything they have experienced before, what they and their narcissist partner have.

They are misled into thinking that all the best relationships are explosive and passionate and that this is a sign that theirs is something very precious. The victim becomes convinced of this "fact" and, thus, finds it more difficult to break things off with every passing day.

I Didn't Mean It / I Was Only kidding

Another way a narcissist will inflict their spitefulness on their victims is to constantly dismiss insults or criticism by claiming they were not really meaning them. They know full well that the initial comment will injure their prey, but make their excuses to cover up their malicious intent. They say they've been joking, but in reality they've been crafty on the offensive to maneuver into a dominant position.

This kind of language further requires the victim to accept the behavior of the narcissist. It confuses them and makes them uncertain as to whether to offend them or not. Not knowing when to look at a comment as an insult and when to take it as a joke simply gives the narcissist power to say what he likes.

Aiming At Defects And Insecurities

A narcissist has an unusual ability to tease out the insecurities of a person and identify all the things the other person considers to be flaws. For such things, they also have a brilliant memory and an almost perfect timing when it comes to using them against their victims. In their questioning, they may even be blunt, using the intimacy and vulnerability cover to pull down any defenses they might encounter. To the victim, it feels like a way to build and reinforce the bond that has been built up so far, but to the narcissist, it's a way to build up their ammunition store for later use.

They will launch an offensive when the time comes, using the information that you trustfully handed over to reopen old wounds and make you feel the same trauma and pain that you have associated with throughout your life. The narcissist thrives on the power they hold over you and is not afraid to use it in any situation they feel their cause is advancing.

Fabricated Praise And Genuine Criticism

It is a skill that most narcissists have to come across as nice, charming, and even complimentary. When it suits them, they can lavish praise on others, but not a single word of it is sincere and honest. Instead, they use false praise to manipulate others, bring them to the side, and make the following criticism more palatable. They might say things like "I like your dress, but it doesn't really flatter your figure" as a way to soften the blow while still digging.

It may look like honesty, but it's all but that. The compliment is nothing short of a lie—something they don't believe in themselves, but it serves their purpose. This is another example of implicit abuse; something that may not always seem so bad for both the victim and the onlookers, but it has a cumulative and harmful effect on the self-esteem of the targets.

Projection

Unwanted, vile, and malicious thoughts and actions of a narcissist are not things they want to see in themselves. These are projected onto their victim to overcome this as a way to shift the issue to someone else. They unleash a barrage of words designed to persuade the other person of their wrongdoing, to bamboozle them into believing that they did wrong even when they did not.

They make charges like "you're paranoid" or "you're a freak of control" to mirror their own problems and transplant them into their victims' beliefs. They repeat this over and over again, with such conviction that the other person ends up thinking that they actually embody these traits or perpetrate some wrongdoing.

Gaslighting

The more their victim can be confused by a narcissist, the easier it becomes to bend them to their will. They will embark on a trickery and deceit campaign that will slowly persuade their prey to lose their minds. The narcissist can effectively write his own script by blurring the other person's perception of reality and know it will be accepted as truth.

They will constantly question the memory of their victim and insist that events have been different from what is being remembered. They will withhold information or manipulate the truth to create the other person's doubt and confusion. The goal is to make the victim feel increasingly dependent on them and less likely to leave.

They might say something along the lines of "thanks for taking this morning's trash out," even though they are fully aware that they have done it themselves. When the other person responds by saying they didn't take it out, the narcissist will insist they had to do it because they certainly didn't, and it didn't move on its own. A small thing, maybe, but it can be incredibly disorientating for the victim when this scene is repeated over and over.

Silence, Volume, And Tone

Sometimes pursuing a silent approach is the most powerful use of language that a narcissist can use. They may simply choose to glare, frown, shake their heads, or turn away during a confrontation.

Alternatively, they may change their voice volume to change the way they communicate their message. Either change is a demonstration of the malice bubbling away beneath the surface.

They may also change the tone in which they speak to convey their words with a different meaning. When on the defensive, they may speak slightly higher or place special emphasis on certain words to push their agenda forward.

These language manipulations–and so on –are intended to exert influence and control over the victim.

A narcissist will take whatever approach is necessary to continue their war of attrition, wearing the other person down in a non-stop mental assault. Identifying these tactics is only the first step in overcoming them and getting rid of the hold that a narcissistic abuser has on you.

Chapter 13
THE LAW OF GRANDIOSITY; THE NARCISSISTS ADDICTION

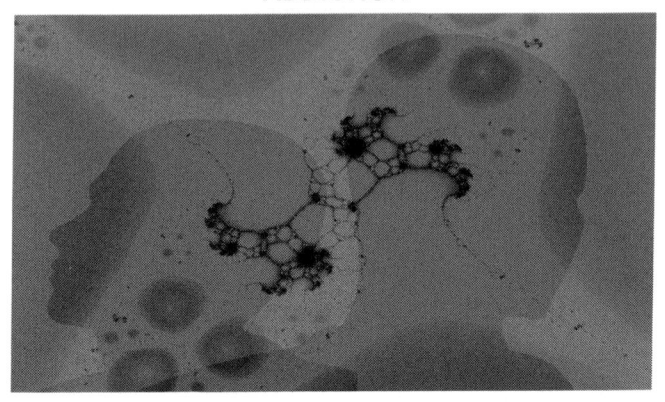

Grandiosity is usually the most remarkable and discriminating feature of Narcissistic Personality Disorder individuals. Grandiosity can be expressed in an unrealistic overvaluation of talents and abilities; concern for unlimited beauty, power, wealth or success fantasies; and belief in unrealistic superiority and uniqueness. This is usually accompanied by behavior that is boastful, pretentious, self-centered and self-referential. The research shows, according to Gunderson and Ronningstam, from "The Diagnostic Interview for Narcissistic Patients" (Archives of General

Psychiatry, 1990), that the grandiose narcissist exaggerates his talents, abilities and achievements in an unrealistic manner. He believes or does not recognize his limitations in his invulnerability. His grandiose fantasies lead him to believe that other people are not needed.

The narcissist seeks admiration and attention in his interpersonal relationships. When he selects someone as the source of his attention, at first he idealizes them unrealistically (they are "all good"), but very soon he usually ends up devaluing them (they become "all bad"), then they end up having feelings of contempt for that person before long. He acts as if he has the right to things, and he has unreasonable expectations of special treatment, and if his demands are not met for any reason, then he becomes hurt and enraged.

He appears or conducts toward people in an arrogant, haughty, or condescending manner, and if he gets the opportunity to exploit them then he will, usually passively, indirectly, or manipulatively, without any intention of reciprocating in any way. He lacks complete empathy (is incapable of understanding and feeling for the experience of other people). The most important characteristic of the narcissistic individual is his inability to maintain satisfactory, mutual and enduring committed relationships. Often they see others either as a means of ego inflation and self-esteem support, or as stepping stones to achieve their own goals. He is hypersensitive when the narcissist is reactive. He responds to any critique or defeat with intense anger. He is very envious of the successes of anyone, no matter how small the success is, and he believes that everyone is envious of him.

The narcissist's Affects and Mood States show he has sustained boredom, meaninglessness, futility, and hollowness feelings. Often he feels impoverished emotionally: yearns for deeper emotional experiences. The grandiose narcissist's social and moral adaptation shows he has superficial and changing values and interests, and shows disregard for unusual / conventional values or societal rules, resulting in corruptible moral and ethical standards. He has broken laws under enraged circumstances or as a way to avoid defeat. He frequently exhibits sexual behavior involving perversion, promiscuity, and/or lack of inhibitions.

So, as you can see from the above research, grandiosity takes place when a person has an inflated self-esteem, believing that they have special powers, spiritual connections, or religious relations. A grandiose individual feels powerful, important, and invincible unrealistically. These beliefs are often accompanied by euphoria and intense pleasure. Nothing seems impossible, each problem has a solution, and the individual may feel an urgent need to initiate projects or activities. The grandiose individual seems pompous, boastful, exaggerated, impulsive, conceited, condescending, and unrealistic to the observer. The failure of grandiose behavior can be devastating, especially when compounded by a Narcissistic Disorder of Personality. High - risk behavior, inflated self - esteem, and delusions often result in job loss, school expulsion, and endless relationships that end.

The narcissist differs from a normal person by living out of such an unrealistic False Self and such a sadistic Superego that he can never reach his highly unrealistic view of his own abilities. As a result, his accomplishments differ from his grandiose fantasies and inflated self-image. This is called The Great Gap (Vaknin). This gap is so staggering that it is unbearable in the long run because it imposes excessive difficulties on the grasp of reality and social skills by the narcissist. His surreal distortions push him either to withdraw from the world or to become furious about acquiring possessions—cars, sex, property, wealth, and power. Regardless of how successful the narcissist becomes, they often end up (in their minds) being abject failures–because it is impossible to bridge the Grandiosity Gap.

In his own fantasy, the narcissist is always a slave. And depending on the individual's circumstances, their grandiose fantasies are likely to cause either inertia (with a dread to move) or acceleration (moving at high speed). On the way to dizzier height and greener pastures, some narcissists are accelerating forever. While others succumb to a state of inertia in which their action appears to freeze, they only spend the minimal amount of energy that they target as a way to exist. But either way, the narcissist's life is out of control, at the mercy of heartless inner voices and internal forces. Underneath all this, there is a Generalized Anxiety eating away at them.

The narcissist believes in his own illusions and is blind to being able to see through them by others. For those people outside the Narcissistic Supply circle, they see the games being played, losing respect for him, they wisely give a wide berth to the narcissist. The narcissist blindly lives in his ivory tower, impervious in his armor of grandiosity, where he believes he is tremendously impressive to everyone. In his exaggerated delusional fantasies of wealth, power, or omnipotence, he displays his grandiosity daily. He's such a megalomaniac that whatever he's talking about (whether it's work, family, possessions, health, accomplishments, etc.) he's always celebrating because he's the shining star in all his stories. He is attributed to any success that another person has in his story; he is the one who takes responsibility for his family, his home, his company, because everyone else is unreliable, uncooperative, or incompetent. Although he manipulates a lot of people to do things for him, he constantly complains that no one is ever helping him. He then goes on to denigrate their abilities and contributions, having received help from others.

All this is done to inspire more self-willed sympathy or admiration that he desires. If you ever had a chance in his Kingdom to visit him, you would find that everyone around him not only pulls their weight, but also carries the share of narcissists. Once you understand your personality, it's easy to see that the addiction to grandiosity of the narcissist is linked to his strong susceptibility to shame. The shame is in relation to failed aspirations and ideals, plaguing and unsatisfactory early object relationships, and narcissistic manifestations with shame at their core. Their inability to process their shame in a healthy way means that they are unable to face up to it, and neutralize it so that they can move on to become a healthier individual. It is this inability that leads to the characteristic postures, attitudes, and behavior of the Grandiose Narcissist.

In the grandiose behavior you might ask, what is the intelligence at work? The intelligence behind the narcissist's grandiose behavior is that it masks profound problems of self-esteem and helps stay away from the hurt and shameful feeling that plagues him so deeply. It also helps him build and maintain his image of being powerful, talented, and desirable, because he is genuinely afraid of being worthless. Any slight or rejection, even involuntary, disturbs his image of himself, throwing him into a fit of anger and depression. Any failure or loss of any kind calls his specialty into question for him. Predictability, he has trouble in his working relationships and personal relationships because he perceives that others fail to appreciate him sufficiently, and when this happens, he tends to react in an arrogant and manipulative manner that further damages relationship. Part of the grandiose behavior is seductive, and this puts him at the center of the attention of the other person. He speaks of casual acquaintances as close friends and of friends as if they are intimate partners, and if he should feel slight or dismissed with these people in any way, then he throws temper tantrums or makes threats of retribution (which he will perform). He doesn't care about others because he's anti-social, except to the extent that he can exploit people to his own ends.

Chapter 14

LETTING GO OF ANGER YOU ARE FEELING TOWARDS YOURSELF

Anger is an immediate reaction to an obstacle. It is a strong negative emotion of displeasure, hostility or fury that might occur to anyone on any occasion. Anger generates other bad feelings such as fear, disgust, shame, irritability, outrage, hostility and even violence and the aggressive response it generates can harm you. Anger is a punishment to you for somebody's fault.

Anger changes the behavior pattern of the person as a result of changes in his emotional status. it is accompanied by physiological and biological changes.

Actions resulting from anger often lead to undesirable physiological and health consequences, because the neuro-transmitters/hormones (eg. adrenaline) released during anger intensify impulsive action and obscure rational thought processes. It may raise your heart rate, the blood pressure and may result in hot reactions. If you hold on to anger so long it will give you tense muscles, stress and unhappiness. Anger is a silent killer. According to Mark Twain anger is an acid that can do more harm to the vessel in which it is stored than to anything on which it is poured.

Anger can lead to problems at home, at work and elsewhere. It spoils the quality of your life wherever you are. Anger can destroy your relationship with your spouse, colleagues and others. The degree of your anger, the manifestation of it and the length of you staying in anger, need skillful management to avoid further problems. We can be angry on the right grounds, against the right persons, in the right manner at the right moment for the right length of time. But remember not to cross those borderlines any time.

Narcissists are trying to get rid of every last shred of your self-esteem because that's how they keep you hooked... to keep you thinking, "I'm damaged goods. It's better for someone to treat me like crap than nobody at all. Remember, most of the things that come out of their mouth are a lie, including the negative things they say about you. Any emotion in the sun. The feelings of chaoticism. Amazing ambivalence. Anger, hatred, vengeance, murder, all things that are really nasty. Terrible loneliness of the soul-tearing. That's normal, you're human. Feel all the emotions, weep an ocean. This is a matter of grief. Anger is uncomfortable, but healing is a necessary step. It feels like an erupting volcano at first, but then it decreases and you can concentrate on how to get through.

Recognizing and admitting that you are angry. Uncovering your feelings is essential, so you can start the healing process. Know where the wrath comes from within you. Repressed emotions are harmful, keeping you trapped and powerless to face the situation or feel happy. Recognizing anger, usually disguised as depression, allows you to decide and deal with what to do about it.

Please reiterate that this was not a natural person, it was a lie, that it was nothing to do with you (the most difficult), but it happened to you ; it is psychological and not because of the disturbed nature of the psychopaths in a mysterious class, not really from this world as we know it. This is a matter of fact.

Hang out with people who support you emotionally but don't make you doubt yourself — people who try to tell you or imply that you're at fault somehow — do not trust anyone who pathologizes your behavior or brings you theories of pathology — a disordered psychopathic character is a relationship anomaly / aberration — normal rules don't apply and theories don't apply.

You remain attached as long as you continue to psychologize about this (non)relationship. Know that you have no control over the encounter, that you have no control over anything except what you choose to believe and choose to elevate all around you. Choose a good life.

Learning how to deal with anger like an intelligent, rational adult can eliminate a lot of drama from your life.

Deal with anger effectively and avoid making a situation even worse:

1. **Take a breath**. It's simple, but effective. Focusing on your breathing takes your mind off the issues that triggered you to get angry... and in doing so, calms you down.

Try this if you're angry: slowly, take in a deep breath through your nose. Hold it for 5 seconds. Then, just as slowly, breathe out through your mouth.

Repeat this process at least 10 times, or until you feel calmer.

2. **Count to 10**. Yes, you've probably heard it a million times, but it wouldn't be repeated if it didn't work. Similar to the breathing technique, one reason 'counting' is effective is because it helps to distract your mind from what you were angry about.

The next time you're feeling angry, count to 10 in a calm and slow manner. For example: 1, 1000... 2, 1000... 3, 1000... and so on. Repeat or vary this process as you see fit, until you feel better.

3. **Change your perception**. Another way to put this technique is to 'look at things from another angle.' When we're angry, we tend to look at things from only one point of view... our own perspective. Instead, try evaluating all the other aspects of a situation. This way you start taking more control over how you feel, rather than giving someone or something else control over your emotions.

4. **Start Laughing**. Laughing raises endorphin levels, which in essence helps us to feel good. Sometimes we

take things, or even ourselves, way too seriously. The next time you feel angry, think of a joke, a funny incident you encountered, or funny part you saw on a TV show... and just laugh. You'll feel better.

5. **Think before you speak**. This is related to tip #3 on the list (changing your perception). Many times when dealing with anger, we make matters worse, because we act on impulse; which in the case of being angry, normally results in escalating problems. This, in turn, only makes us angrier... which makes us act on impulse... which makes us angrier... which makes us act on impulse... which makes us... okay, you get the point. Take the time to think before you speak or act.

6. **Take a hike**. Not literally of course... unless you like hiking. But consider walking away from the situation that's getting you angry, for a few minutes. This way you give yourself the opportunity to calm down, and assess the situation in a more rational state of mind. This will be a good time to practice some of the other techniques on this list.

7. Ask yourself, "what am I angry at?" Once you have the answer to that, then ask yourself, "why am I angry?" The purpose of these two questions are to shift your mindset from 'feeling' the anger, into 'thinking' about the anger. Which in turn helps you to change your focus... and think things through.

When you get angry, think whether that element of anger is inevitable. We can consciously train ourselves to tolerate frustration or irritation without getting angry too much. You can deal with anger by accepting things and events as they are and realizing that you cannot change all the situations or individuals that irritate you. If you are angry, admit it to yourself and avoid prolonging it. Prolonging anger can lead you to self-destruction or self-defeat. Do not stay back with anger so long. Think of ways to express it constructively. You can express your anger to anyone who triggered your anger directly or over phone or in writing. But ensure that your reaction is calm, assertive and not aggressive. Aggressive way may escalate your hurt feelings. As well, if you feel so angry, you can talk your reactions to yourself or to any another person or even to a pet to unburden yourself and to discharge the anger. Don't postpone this till when you have overcome the anger and are feeling good later. Physical ventilation or exertion can drain off your anger. Do exercise, sports or physical activity to reduce anger. Mediate regularly to overcome anger overload.

The positive aspect of anger is that it helps us to recognize something is wrong somewhere. But don't get angry on anything and everything. When you get angry, choose to let it off, take a few breaths, or countdown to ten, or analyses why you are upset. Realizing that you are caught with anger is the right way to begin to deal with it. All your anger is about something what has happened in the past or will happen in the future and not what is happening in the present moment. So if you can be in the present moment you cannot hold on to anger for long. So be in the present moment to avoid holding on to anger. Physical exercises can relieve your anger.

Let us look at the Kids. They get angry anytime and manage it beautifully. When they are in anger, they express their feelings openly, directly and allow it to go. Within minutes, they can start laughing, playing and leaving the anger behind by choosing to 'live in the present moment'. Nurture the nature of a child to deal with anger.

Anger will affect the quality of your life and the productivity at work. If you don't do anything about managing your anger, it will cause problems to you, and others in the society in which you live. The best way to deal with anger is to understand the nuances of anger. Manage it skillfully and lead a happier life.

Chapter 15
THE SOLUTION; PROVEN METHOD TO HELP YOU RECOVER FROM NARCISSISTIC ABUSE

When you set out to get rid of the hold that the narcissist has on you in your life and the painful memories that seem to haunt you day after day, it's helpful to have some steps of things you can do to help you break free.

When I went through the breaking-up phase of the narcissistic relationship and the crumbling illusion of what I thought was true, I knew that I had very little energy to do anything. I was just going to lie down and die. This is a common apathy we find ourselves in after the narcissistic abuse comes with discarding and devaluation.

Usually our life force energy leaves us feeling alone, worthless and depleted. There is an intense pain of rejection and an even more intense disbelief. We don't want the painful truth to believe, so we're telling ourselves stories that make us feel better.

In the long run, however, dwelling on these stories makes us feel worse. The biblical phrase "The Truth Set You Free" you may have heard! "The longer we continue to deny the longer the pain stays with us.

The sooner we face the reality of our situation, the sooner we can move beyond the illusion in which we lived with the narcissist and the sooner we can live a real life, sometimes for the very first time ever!

Our life is based on falsehoods when we live in the narcissistic illusion. We are increasingly surrendering our reality to the narcissist's reality, and we are gradually wasting away to a desolate life. Once our energy has been spent, in our lives we are of no use or value to the narcissist. They will either take a vacation from us to give us time to replenish our energy reserves or leave entirely for a more powerful supply source that doesn't need to wait around for you to replenish.

A narcissist hates weakness, and the more powerless you are, the weaker you show him. Your weakness only gives him more fuel and ammunition to attack you physically, emotionally or psychically.

But the truth is the weak is the narcissist. He is the one who, if the truth is told, has such an incredibly low sense of self-worth that in order to survive he had to learn the masterful art of projection. This means that he denies his own weakness, his own insecurity, his own lack of self-worth and focuses these hidden feelings on the people that are closest to him. If he hates himself, he will eventually find something to hate you. He seems to hate everything about you by the time the relationship falls apart.

Yet again, the truth is that he knows you no more than he knows himself. You are a fictional character in his head that he used to project on himself the hidden parts. If I were to describe you as a victim of narcissistic abuse, I would say that she is an inside-out narcissistic personality. This means the narcissist has projected all of her self-hatred and weakness on the victim over a period of time until she comes to believe that she is who she is. She has given herself away little by little, little by little, in exchange for the narcissist's dark inner world.

The role of "The Sin Eater" for the narcissist is unknowingly assigned to victims of narcissism. He uses his victims as a scapegoat to dump all of his sins on himself or to dump everything that he denies. The victims of narcissism become heavily burdened with these sins or projections over a period of time, and the heavier the narcissist becomes with them the more disgusted they become.

The final act of sin eating is when the narcissist makes his final dumping on the scapegoat and then throws it out, which we have come to know as being devalued and discarded. The narcissist continues with a new person to have a fresh start and you are left to be the goat of sacrifice. In biblical times, the wealthy people of society used a goat or a lamb to dump their sins on them. Once they transferred their sins to the goat or lamb, according to tradition, it was either slain or sends away.

Using a scapegoat is a very old tradition in our society that still lives. You will find that people with problems with drugs and alcohol are often going to scapegoat their problems on those closest to them. This makes it impossible for them to face their own addictions.

He doesn't want to face his own inadequacy with a narcissistic personality so he projects it on those closest to him. He does this until the narcissist's mind becomes so inadequate that he doesn't even know what he's doing with such a person. He cannot take responsibility for his world's complexity. You are the complex one in his mind, and he has the right to a better life with someone more adequate.

In many cases, before the narcissist does, the victims will leave, but this is out of their own sense of survival. The victim intuitively knows that she must leave to save her own life by this time. She knows intuitively that she is the lamb of sacrifice and has to run fast before the final sacrifice is made. I'm speaking here metaphorically. Few personalities of narcissism are real killers. They're more like violists of the soul. They extract your energy until nothing is left for you to extract. You probably still have your physical body, even though it may be depleted as well.

By the time you realize what has happened to you, it is nearly too late. You are already gone, so to speak. You've given away the best of yourself. But I'm here to tell you that you can get back. It's not over until it's finished. You don't want the narcissist back, it's yourself. Unfortunately, most victims are obsessed with the narcissist, believing it is he they miss and longing for. It's hard for the victim to understand that she's missing the self.

The method I will discuss here is to give you solid ways to detach yourself from the narcissistic entity and recover what has been lost. Read each method carefully and put it into effect in your life, and almost immediately you will notice a difference.

<u>Method One: Bid Farewell To The Narcissist</u>

It is important to leave the situation when you realize you are dealing with a narcissistic personality or any emotionally abusive personality. Get the idea of making it better or changing the person. You can't make anybody change! You are the only person you can change. By refusing to allow yourself to continue being abused, you change yourself. You deserve to be treated with dignity and respect, and sometimes you have to ask yourself for this treatment. They don't deserve to be around you if someone constantly undermines you and belittles you.

The longer you stay the worse it gets with the narcissist. You may have periods of honeymoon, but it will always go back to worse than before. You're living in a fantasy land if you think it's going to change. Coming out of the fantasy is the same as waking up from the illusion under which you have lived. You have to crumble the illusion and face the truth. He's a narcissist, the truth! He is unhappy at the very heart and if you remain connected to him, he will continue to project his unhappiness on you. The sooner you disconnect with him, the sooner you will be able to recover your energy and continue your life.

Yes, he's going to go somewhere else! That's what narcissists are doing. They need a canvas to project on their inadequacies. It'll be someone else if it's not you. Do not envy the period of honeymoon that the new supply source might have with your ex. He's scapegoated you and dumped all the negative qualities within himself that he's repressed so he's apparently got a clean slate to start over. However, the more you purge what he has given you, the more balancing will be the energetic scales and filling up again his well of negativity. Soon, as you once were, the new source will be the target for these repressed emotions. It's just a matter of time.

Yes, he's going to go somewhere else! That's what narcissists are doing. They need a canvas to project on their inadequacies. It'll be someone else if it's not you. Do not envy the period of honeymoon that the new supply source might have with your ex. He's scapegoated you and dumped all the negative qualities within himself that he's repressed so he's apparently got a clean slate to start over. However, the more you purge what he has given you, the more balancing will be the energetic scales and filling up again his well of negativity. Soon, as you once were, the new source will be the target for these repressed emotions. It's just a matter of time.

Think of it like this! The more you reclaim your energy, your power and your sense of self-worth, the more energy you are taking back from him and the more he will be dumping on the new source. It's like an exchange of energy. He's been extracting your energy and using it to seduce the new source. What will he use, though, once your energy is recovered? Hers!

If you sit on your pity pot and say woe is me, he left me with your power for a younger, smarter, slimmer, more attractive mate than you will keep feeding him. You're going to keep feeling something is wrong with you. You're not the issue. He's there! Your problem is you let him dump his B.S. It's on you!

It is time, once and for all, to say goodbye! Let go of him! You might have loved him, of course, and you surely had good times. But it's over! Love you now! Love enough to say NO MORE! Confide in your intuition. Trust that what you know is true inside somewhere deep.

You're a worthy person and you've got a lot to offer. You are able to have a healthy, loving relationship. It's just that you first have to love yourself and have a healthy life relationship. You will attract healthy people into your life once you achieve this and you will be attracted to healthy people.

It's good you're leaving behind the past. Starting fresh is time for you! You're the one that's going to get the better deal! You've got to ride it out! On an energetic level, you have to take back what's yours and then you'll be free of it. But he is still going to have to live with himself. Tell him or her goodbye! Goodbye! Close the gate! Do not reopen it! It's just your way out!

Method Two: Remove All Contact

It has been proven that cutting off all contact with him is the only way to truly detach from the narcissist's dark reality. This means shutting down the doors, the windows, the mailbox, the email box, the instant chat room, the phone, the text message, and any other avenue you might have in or out of your reality.

The cat was killed by curiosity. Don't allow you to control your curiosity. The situation must be monitored. Be satisfied that either anger or manipulation will be what he has to say to you. It's always been that way. No reason to change it now.

Yes, I know that part of you continues to ask if the love was real. Has he ever really loved me? I can answer your question so you don't have to waste your time grasping the narcissist's thrown crumbs. NO! NO! He was unable to love you because he was unable to love himself. He hides himself and the rest of the world. There's no love in it. It doesn't mean that you don't deserve love. You're, of course. You're beautiful. But you also have to work on your self-love.

Your own lack of self-love is what made you bait for the narcissist. You didn't love yourself enough to say NO! Now you must! Your life depends on it!

You have to do it as your life depends on it when you cut off contact with the narcissist. He has a way back in if he knows where you are emotionally or even physically. You must consider yourself dead to him. From this day on, he can't know anything about you. He can't know how you're feeling, what you're doing, whether you care about it or not. I've been told that indifference is the worst thing you can do to a narcissist. For his love, he can take away your pining, and he can take away your anger, but your indifference is more than he can take away. Because indifference means you don't have anything to emotionally react to it. And emotion feeds the narcissist.

Even if you are feeling the worst kind of pain, he need not know a thing. This is between you and your support system.

Write your last letter when you say good-bye. I know I said in my books that cutting off contact does not mean sending letters or emails to the narcissist. But there is benefit in the last time before closing the door, dumping everything he has dumped on you.

Method Three: Get Angry

You are most likely very angry after a long period of abuse, even though you may not be in touch with your anger. It's important to let yourself get angry with everything you want! I was told it wasn't spiritual anger! Yet, for good reason, God gave us our wrath. Our anger detects where we are abused, misused and mistreated. If we keep stuffing our feelings under the rug because they're not the lady we're going to deny ourselves just like the narcissist.

We learn not to show our anger in our relationships with the narcissist. Whenever I got angry, I know that I'm "out of control" or "abusive" or "calm down." He took my concerns up and turned it around to be all about my anger rather than what I was angry about. I may have been angry at his treatment of me and trying to voice my feelings just to focus on my emotional expression rather than the issue at hand.

This is a typical manipulation of narcissism. It's another way of avoiding the problems.

Narcissistic abuse victims have no voice. They are not permitted to express themselves in the relationship unless it is all positive praise for him or an outer objective agreed upon by one another. If the issue is related to the narcissist or the victim's relationship is always shut down. Years of stifling our voices and stuffing under the built-up rug our feelings. The result may be the worst type of depression. This can be very true if you've ever heard that anger turned inward into depression. When we cut off from our emotions, we get numb and depression is the result of all this numbing. Our life force is being suppressed as well as our vitality.

It's so important to get out of the closet with our anger! We have to allow our feelings to be expressed. Voice them in the last letter! Or voice them through a letter that is burned instead of sent if you've already cut off contact. It's important for you to express how lively you are about your treatment. It's important that you drudge and let them come to the surface all the feelings you've been sitting on. It can be a very passionate experience to get in touch with your anger. It can release energy from your life force. It's all right. If you need to scream and scream and throw a tantrum. Don't just take it out on anyone near you. It's not all right. To raise your anger against other innocent people. We already know how dangerous it can be to scapegoat.

If you have a punching bag or pillow, going ahead and releasing your anger by physical means is helpful. I've got a friend who used to take a plastic bat to a pillow and bat the pillow as hard as she could, screaming and screaming. It helped her get out of her anger so that her energy would not be suppressed. Some people use physical exercise to express their anger, such as jogging or working out. Anger requires a lot of adrenaline to be used up. To deal with this excess of adrenaline, exercise is a very healthy way. It's not sitting around eating emotions.

Don't let the narcissist's haunting after voice stop you from getting angry. You deserve to be furious! You were used! You were abused! The narcissist with your feelings was manipulative and careless. Anything he's ever said negative about being angry with all his stuff can be thrown out of the window. You have a good right to be angry and the time has come to express it!

Method Four: Mourn Whatever Has Been Lost

It's good to allow yourself to really experience your grief after expressing your anger. You're bound to feel a deep sense of loss if you've given your heart and soul and love to someone who misused it. If you don't feel he's worth it, it doesn't matter. It's worth it! You've had a death experience. Death is not just the relationship, but the illusion under which your relationship has lived. It wasn't true! It's a painful thing to deal with.

It is a very healthy thing to cry out your eyes. It's good to release all that grief and emotion. After a good cry, you always feel so much better. It's as if you've been purging deep inside.

Learn about the normal stages of grief as described by Kubler-Ross.

The stages are:

1. **Denial**: The initial stage: "It can't be happening."
2. **Anger**: "Why me? It's not fair."
3. **Bargaining**: "Just let me live to see my children graduate."
4. **Depression**: "I'm so sad, why bother with anything?"
5. **Acceptance**: "It's going to be OK."

I think people often bounce a little bit around the stages. One may experience depression before anger, for example. That's meaningful. If suppressed anger results in depression, then experiencing depression would be normal and then anger would move one out of depression.

The important thing is to really feel your feelings for yourself. If you have to wear black for a while and hibernate indoors, so be it! Just be careful not to spend more than three months doing this. Starting to interact with life again is important at some point, even if you don't feel like it. Once you get out, you'll feel much better.

It's important to be aware that you're in a process of grief. You might want a burial ceremony and bury a box of stuff that reminds you of the narcissist or even burns them in a bonfire, a fireplace or some other way. You may want to collect all cards, letters, or anything that is a reminder and dispose of them on a ceremonial basis.

Method Five: Cut The Psychic Bonds

Our energy fields merge when we bond with a narcissist. Imagine an invisible energy web that ties you to the narcissist. It is by merging these fields that the extraction of your energy is so easy for a narcissist. After all, he's got access to your energy field. When a psychic intuitive person reads, they simply tap into their field of energy and read whatever impressions they take on. She can do this because through thought we are all connected. The act of thinking about someone will enable you to access their field of energy.

It is very important to cut the energetic chords that run in your life between you and the narcissist to free up your energy and separate you from it. If your energy is still merging with his, even long after the physical relationship is over, he can continue to feed on it. It is a relatively simple yet very invisible process to cut the energy chords between you and the narcissist. Although you may feel them, you don't see immediate results. It is good to set it up as a ceremony before performing a chord cut. If you have it, light candles, burn sage or incense, and become comfortable and relaxed, lying down preferably.

Imagine being surrounded by a cocoon of brilliant white light that creates a protective field around you and protects you from any non-harmonious energy. It's always good to immerse yourself in a bath of sea salt once you perform the chord cutting ceremony, which is known to help clear negative energy. Simply add half a cup of sea salt to your bath water and soak for at least 20 minutes. Remember, by letting him back in the door in one way or another, you can easily invite the negative chords to reattach themselves. In order to be completely clear, you may have to perform the ceremony several times.

Method Six: Take Care Of Yourself

Sometimes it's the hardest time to take care of yourself when you feel the most down and out and depressed. Yet this is also when focusing on caring for yourself is the most important time. Now is the time to eat well, get plenty of fresh air and exercise. It's important to take time to read things you enjoy reading, soak up candles, hot baths, good music, and special treatments. It's very important the food you eat. Food is no longer of very poor quality in our society. It is loaded with toxins, chemicals, and various poisons that affect your body's chemical balance, health, and moods.

Just changing your diet alone could have a huge impact on how you feel about yourself. The first thing to do is to cut out all processed foods when changing your diet. This means eliminating all white sugar, white flour, table salt, fried foods, and most foods in a box, a bag, or a can. Eliminate fast food and make food convenient. Even though it may be hard at first, once you make this change, you will feel so much better and it gives you another place to focus your energy.

What are you going to eat? Focus on buying nutrition of high quality, even if you don't eat it. Eat lots of fresh, preferably raw and preferably organic fruits and vegetables. Organic is more expensive but much better to taste and has so much more energy in terms of nutrition and life force. This is because chemicals, pesticides, herbicides and radiation have not been treated. These things are destroying the value of food.

Indeed, many people starve for nutrition and do not realize it. Even those who are obese may be hungry. Fat is not equal to nutrition on the body. It's important to be sure that you get high-quality nutrition in your body when you take good care of yourself. Study nutrition and natural hygiene for raw and living foods.

A great addition to your diet is an abundance of natural live organic foods such as fruits, vegetables, nuts, seeds, nutbutters, sea vegetables and live juices. Whole grains, legumes and natural sweeters such as honey, real maple syrup, agave nectar and stevia can be added. Drink purified water and herbal teas, eliminating all of the market's artificial drinks.

I know it's a real challenge for most of you to change your diet, but what better time to take care of yourself. Focusing on you and doing something that will make you feel much better about yourself, have so much more energy, and even look ten years younger is an excellent time.

<u>Exercise</u>

Another important way of taking care of yourself is exercise. It is very good for the body to learn yoga, go for walks or even jump on a rebounder or trampoline and release energy. Yoga will help you to restore energy to your life force.

Meditation

It is an important exercise to do on a daily basis to meditate or sit in silence. We're getting so busy with our minds that we're not giving them enough quiet time. It is extremely beneficial for your body, mind and spirit to sit quietly in silence and focus on your breathing. Give yourself to be quiet and breathe twice a day for at least ten minutes.

Taking hot salt water baths or baths with essential oils

Taking baths with hot salt water or baths with essential oils is a great way to eat, clean and relax. I often combine my bath time with my meditation. Lying back in a fragrant pool of warm water, burning candles and just being.

Writing in a journal

Writing in a journal is a great exercise to do on a daily basis. It helps you to get in touch with your feelings and emotions and to be in the moment. If you don't already have a journal you may want to purchase one and keep it near for those times you just need to express yourself.

Being in nature

Being in nature is an important thing to do in your healing process. Nature is a healer and the more time you immerse yourself in it the more you will experience its healing. Go for walks in nature, sit by a stream, listen to the birds, gaze at a blooming flower, watch an animal or whatever presents itself. I know in the warmer weather I am always outdoors hiking in beautiful natural places. It always seems to restore my energy and a strong sense of peace.

Take time for you

All the above requires a time commitment. Now is the very best time to take for yourself. Make yourself important. Do nice things for you. Buy yourself little gifts, get a message, purchase higher quality food, take time to do yoga, write, meditate and all the good things you can do for yourself.

Now is also a great time to study new things, especially in the areas of personal and spiritual growth. Become a student, take classes, read, write and learn. Take the lemons you have been given and make lemonade.

Method Seven: Get Out Into The World

It only serves you so long to stay home in hibernation. There comes a time when step back into the world is important. You're only going to step out in a whole new way this time. Get out with the idea of getting in touch with other positive people on a conscious path of growth. You can do this through centers, classes, and support groups of spiritual growth.

It would be a good way to enter the world and do something beneficial to volunteer your time for a cause you believe in. You might be able to volunteer in a shelter for women or work with the homeless. Getting out and working with those who are less fortunate than yourself sometimes helps you realize you don't have it that bad. Your compassion for others will come in very handy and you will feel good knowing you are contributing to life in a positive way.

If you struggle to get out or take the next step in your life, it may be a good time to seek therapy or get some help. It would be wise to find someone knowledgeable about narcissistic abuse if you get any kind of counseling. For an eye problem, we wouldn't go to a dentist. Some therapists are as familiar with narcissism as they are with dentistry that may not be very empowering to you.

If you're working a full-time job, you might feel too exhausted to volunteer your time elsewhere, but you might find it better to volunteer on a Saturday than to sit alone and think. Getting out of our heads sometimes is a really good idea. Too much sitting at home gives us the chance to dwell and obsess with what happened. While it is important to take quiet time, too much can be futile.

Take yourself out to a movie, or to a nice restaurant. Meet some new people who could go with you. Take a mini vacation to a bed and breakfast or a retreat center. Learn to ride a motorcycle or a horse. Learn to roller blade or ski. It's never too late to learn something new.

If you enjoy writing you may want to take a writing class and work on that novel you've always wanted to write.

Getting back to life and doing the things you've always wanted to do is a great time. Make a list of things! What would you enjoy doing? What'd stop you from doing it? See if you can't find ways around your life's obstacles and start living in ways you've never allowed yourself to live.

Don't worry about being seen! Don't worry about being heard! Don't be afraid in this life to take up space. For a reason you were born and you deserve to be here! Live the way you mean life. Good things. Intend to happen. The way you want it to be to live your life. Intend to have loving relationships and partnerships. Talk to yourself positively and stop any negative chatter. Stop obsessing with the past and concentrate on creating a new future.

Life is what you really do. Forgive yourself for your past sins for allowing yourself to be badly treated. Yesterday you can let go of it now! It's a new day today! Completely embrace it and refuse to let yesterday's burdens now rob you of your life.

Chapter 16

CONCLUSION

They wore a mask of deception, but once you are entangled in a relationship with them you begin to see it clearly. Again, part of the trauma of breaking up with a Narcissist is they presented so differently than what you experienced from the beginning to when their cracks began to show. Those who are not close enough to the Narcissist doesn't necessarily see this pattern, so may be very surprised if you were to share what you went through in a relationship with them.

That is why it is often best to know this in advance. If you are ready to heal you must learn about yourself, your childhood trauma, you must learn boundary setting and be able to understand your accountability and above ALL you must heal the PTSD. What a narcissist did to you is only half the story, the other half is your own issues as to why you stayed, why you allowed yourself to be treated this badly.

Note this not like the blaming from a friend that doesn't understand more of a self-exploration, remember a narcissist will not take accountability for anything, as survivors we need to understand this and make peace with it.

What we didn't know did hurt us, so now we must learn and protect ourselves so this never happens again.

If you're in a relationship with a narcissist, it's important to seek professional help and support to rebuild your confidence and restore your self-esteem. Keep in mind that you are better than you think you are – the NPD person's constant badgering has broken down your self-confidence and made you feel unworthy, but you aren't – you are a victim of abuse.

Find a mental health professional who is specially trained in trauma recovery to aid in healing from narcissistic abuse. If you are unable to leave the relationship, a therapist can help you learn to communicate effectively and set boundaries so the narcissist can no longer take advantage of you.

Do not go yet; One last thing to do

If you enjoyed this book or found it useful I'd be very grateful if you'd post a short review on Amazon. Your support really does make a difference and I read all the reviews personally so I can get your feedback and make this book even better.

Thanks again for your support!

*© Copyright 2019 by **THERESA MILLER***

<u>All rights reserved</u>

Manufactured by Amazon.ca
Bolton, ON